THE SUGAR-FREE COOKBOOK

THE SUGAR-FREE COOKBOOK

Easy, Healthy, and Sugar-Free Recipes

Breakfast • Lunch • Dinner • Dessert • Snacks

This edition published by Cottage Door Press, LLC, in 2019.
First published 2016 by Parragon Books, Ltd.

5005 Newport Drive, Rolling Meadows, Illinois 60008

New recipes and food styling by Georgina Besterman
Created and produced by Pene Parker and Becca Spry
New photography by Haarala Hamilton
The cover shows Blueberry and Oat Breakfast Bars (32); Warm Quinoa, Roasted Squash, and Pine Nut Salad (50); Hearty Beef Stew with Herbed Cheese Dumplings and Kale (78); and Raspberry and Mascarpone Ice Cream (120).

ISBN: 978-1-68052-898-5

Printed in China

Love Food™ is an imprint of Cottage Door Press, LLC.
Parragon Books® and the Parragon® logo are registered trademarks of Cottage Door Press, LLC.

Notes for the Reader

This book uses standard kitchen measuring spoons and cups. All spoon and cup measurements are level unless otherwise indicated. Unless otherwise stated, milk is assumed to be whole, eggs are large, individual vegetables are medium, and pepper is freshly ground black pepper. Unless otherwise stated, all root vegetables should be peeled prior to using. People with nut allergies should be aware that some of the prepared ingredients used in the recipes in this book may contain nuts.

Garnishes, decorations, and serving suggestions are all optional and not necessarily included in the recipe ingredients or method. The times given are only an approximate guide. Preparation times differ according to the techniques used by different people and the cooking times may also vary from those given. Optional ingredients, variations, or serving suggestions have not been included in the time calculations.

While the author has made all reasonable efforts to ensure that the information contained in this book is accurate and up to date at the time of publication, anyone reading this book should note the following important points: Medical and pharmaceutical knowledge is constantly changing and the author and the publisher cannot and do not guarantee the accuracy or appropriateness of the contents of this book; In any event, this book is not intended to be, and should not be relied upon, as a substitute for appropriate, tailored professional advice. Both the author and the publisher strongly recommend that a physician or other healthcare professional is consulted before embarking on major dietary changes; For the reasons set out above, and to the fullest extent permitted by law, the author and publisher: (i) cannot and do not accept any legal duty of care or responsibility in relation to the accuracy or appropriateness of the contents of this book, even where expressed as "advice" or using other words to this effect; and (ii) disclaim any liability, loss, damage, or risk that may be claimed or incurred as a consequence—directly or indirectly—of the use and/or application of any of the contents of this book.

CONTENTS

INTRODUCTION

Sugar seems to be in almost everything we eat, from prepared meals to natural ingredients such as fruit and vegetables. It is thought that many of us consume ten or more teaspoons of sugar every day. The negative impact of this high-sugar diet on our health is increasingly evident in the rising levels of obesity.

A sugary diet may be a factor in causing type 2 diabetes, and for those who have diabetes, a diet low in sugar will help them maintain a healthy weight and reduce the risk of medical complications. It is also thought that sleep disturbances and mood disorders can also be linked to overindulgence in sugar. Health issues aside, a sugar binge can quickly be followed by a "crash," where your energy levels plummet, leaving you feeling exhausted.

To understand your overall intake of sugar you need to look beyond the quantity of packet sugar that you use from day to day to products that you buy regularly that have significant amounts of "hidden" sugar. Products with hidden sources of sugar range from mayonnaise and salad dressing to pasta sauces, soup, and fruit yogurts.

This book is about becoming aware of where sugar is found, both openly and concealed, within day-to-day cooking, and then taking action to avoid it. The problems aren't only associated with refined sugars; sugar is sugar after all, and natural sugars need to be restricted, too, in particular those containing fructose (see page 9).

In this book, you'll find sugar-free or low-sugar versions of the things you love to eat, such as Coffee and Pecan Mini Breakfast Muffins on page 30, a reduced-tomato Italian Meat Sauce on page 81, and Black Rice Risotto with Prosciutto and Charred Endive on page 82. However, no one wants to have their favorite foods adapted so much that they bear no resemblance to the original. If you bake a cake, then you want to end up with something that looks and tastes like a cake. The Zucchini Loaf Cake with Cream Cheese Frosting on page 110 and the Sweet Potato Brownies on page 112 are sure to delight cake lovers.

Of course, you probably won't eradicate all sugar from your diet; it would be unrealistic and inadvisable to stop eating all fruit permanently, for example. However, the recipes in this book include no more than six grams of sugar per three and a half ounces (or one hundred grams) of ingredients. If you keep your intake to this low-to-negligible level, you can be confident that you are managing your sugars well.

WHAT IS FRUCTOSE?

Sugar, or sucrose as it is scientifically known, comes in the chemical forms of glucose and fructose. Glucose is the basic stuff of life, and every single cell in every single thing growing or moving produces and uses it. We do not need to go out of our way to consume glucose because the body's digestive system releases it from a lot of foods. Fructose is the simplest form of carbohydrate and is about one-and-a-fifth times the sweetness of table sugar.

Throughout human evolution, fructose was only periodically available in especially ripe fruit and some vegetables and nuts. The human body can handle small amounts of fructose very well, but is not designed to deal with it in large amounts, so it can be damaging if we eat too much. While every cell in the body is slurping up glucose, only the liver can process fructose in significant amounts. If the liver is overloaded with fructose, it converts it straight into fat, which results in weight gain and has been linked to obesity, type 2 diabetes, heart disease, and even cancer.

A further problem with fructose is that while some natural sugars stimulate the release of insulin in the body, fructose sneaks under our natural radar system. Fructose has a slower rate of uptake than glucose and doesn't make you feel full in the same way. It also contains the hormone "grehlin," which keeps us feeling hungry. This results in a tendency to eat a greater number of calories if any part of what you are eating contains fructose. Also, once fructose arrives in the liver, it can provide glycerol, the backbone of fat, and increase fat formation, leading to weight gain and the danger of associated diseases.

Fructose is hiding in many day-to-day foods, from some prepared meals and diet products to sugary drinks. It is also found naturally in fruit and vegetables. Many of us feel we are making a healthy choice if we reach for an apple or raw carrot, but it is important to limit how much high-sugar fruit and vegetables we eat, too. While they are nutritious, the sugar they contain quickly adds up.

Most fructose is consumed in liquid form, such as in carbonated drinks and other sweet drinks, and so is not connected to other sources of carbohydrate, which increases any negative metabolic effects. Naturally occurring fruit sugars, in contrast, are bonded together, and so the impact of the fructose intake is reduced.

HIDDEN SUGARS

Sugar might not be as easy to detect as you think it is. Even when you know that a product contains sugar, the amount that it contains can still be surprising. An average can of soft drink is estimated to have around seven teaspoons of sugar and ready made pasta sauces can include up to half an ounce of sugar per serving.

It is advisable to check the packaging when buying any prepared food products. On the front of the packet it may advertise the food's fat and calorie content, but you usually need to check the back for sugars. Often, when the fat is removed from a product, sugar is added to enhance the flavor. Look for the section of the nutrition label for "total carbohydrates"; beneath that it should say how much of these are "sugars." You should also keep an eye out for dextrose, honey, glucose, and maltose in the products you are buying—these are variations on sugar and can be equally detrimental to our health.

The best way to effectively control your sugar intake is to prepare homemade food using a good balance of fresh ingredients as often as possible. This way, you will know the exact ingredients that are going into your meals and you can avoid sugar-laden products by carefully checking your food labels.

Yet even natural foods can have potential pitfalls. Many foods from nature, including most fruit, are full of sugar. If you want to cut out sugar, fruit juice and dried fruit should also be avoided. Vegetables can also have a high-sugar content; sugar snap peas, artichokes, and beets are just some of the vegetables that are high in sugar and should therefore be eaten sparingly. It is also true that the natural sugar in some fruit, including apples, has increased as new varieties have been developed to answer our desire for a sweet fix.

If you are eating a product that does not conveniently come with a helpful breakdown of its nutritional components, simply avoid it if it has a sweet taste, and remember that "low-calorie" does not necessarily mean "low-sugar."

It is also important to look out for refined carbohydrates. The body reacts to most carbohydrates by breaking them down into sugar. Therefore, white flour should be avoided, which means most pastries, breads, and cakes should not be eaten. White rice, noodles, pasta, and potatoes are also off the menu.

GOOD FATS AND PROTEIN

The low-sugar eater has two great allies: protein and fat. Since the 1980s, it has been fashionable to label fat as "the enemy" and carbs as "the good guys." A big bowl of pasta has long been considered a healthy choice. Now, the rise of the low-carb lifestyle has turned these beliefs on their head, and a small portion of whole-wheat pasta is considered a healthy option. If you're keeping your sugar intake down and avoiding refined carbohydrates, you will need protein and fat to replace this energy.

The body naturally produces leptin to regulate and distribute fat. The body's regulatory gland, the hypothalamus, is sensitive to leptin and will tell the brain the stomach is full when there is leptin in the blood, thus suppressing appetite.

The avocado, a food that is naturally low in sugar but loaded with monounsaturated fats, which play a big role in reducing cholesterol, is a good choice for anyone watching their sugar intake. Heroic monounsaturated fats are found all over the food aisles, in products from olive oil and oily fish to animal fats, nuts, and dairy. These foods often contain virtually no sugar, and so are used as the basis for many low-sugar recipes, adding a sense of indulgence to a dish. Of course, as with everything, it is important to manage your intake of foods containing monounsaturated fats; they should be eaten in moderation.

Fat's fondly regarded cousin is protein. Lean meats and eggs have always been in the healthy eater's arsenal, and they can certainly be enjoyed in the sugar-free kitchen. Protein has a marvelous ability to make you feel full; if you eat enough of it, a hormone called PYY is triggered, which is effective in creating a sense of fullness and removing the desire to eat.

Protein-rich products are incredibly diverse. They include meat and fish, dairy products (such as cheese and yogurt), seeds and nuts, and some surprising grains (such as quinoa).

Natural, high-protein ingredients tend to be low in sugar too. However, watch out again for processed products advertising themselves as high protein, as they can also contain hidden sugars used to add extra flavor or texture.

CRASHES AND CRAVINGS

If you would like to avoid energy crashes and sugar cravings in the course of your day, you need to keep your blood sugars as stable as you can. The level of sugar in your blood will increase whenever you eat a large amount of carbohydrates, and if what you are eating is pure sugar, then the effect is compounded.

The best way to avoid blood sugar highs is, therefore, to avoid sugar and large amounts of carbohydrates. Living a low-sugar lifestyle should protect you against energy crashes, which are particularly common midmorning and midafternoon. Sugar crashes occur when sugar quickly enters the bloodstream, making blood sugar levels spike. Then, as the body releases large amounts of insulin to encourage the cells to absorb the glucose, blood glucose levels drop rapidly, leaving you feeling fatigued and lethargic.

You can avoid or reduce blood sugar highs by eating low GI carbohydrates, such as whole-grain bread and rice, which produce natural, slowly released energy. If you also include fat and protein in what you eat, then you will feel fuller for longer. Healthy fats, protein, and fiber contain little if any sugar and provide slow-release energy without having the same effect on the body.

We know that sugar makes you feel good. In fact, a high intake of carbohydrates that includes sugar releases serotonin, the happiness chemical, in the brain. According to research, cravings are simply all in your head. It is thought that the sections of the brain most active during cravings are the parts responsible for memory and sensing pleasure and fulfillment, which suggests that memory and not bodily needs often triggers cravings.

In order to trigger the strong mental sequence that is a craving, the body tends to want (although not need) something, and often that something is sugar after a blood glucose dip. These are the moments when self-control is necessary. It can help to have something on hand to snack on, such as a bag of nuts or piece of cheese. There are some recipes for low-sugar snacks in this book, such as the Crunchy Parmesan and Kale Chips on page 64. You'll also find portable snacking recipes, such as the Chocolate and Brazil Nut Bars on page 66 and the Ginger and Oat No-Bake Cookies on page 70. Responding to cravings by snacking on low-sugar foods such as these will help you through them.

HOW TO STOCK YOUR PANTRY

Sugar is often synonymous with celebration and pleasure. Dessert is the crescendo of a dinner, cake is considered a treat, holidays are associated with sugary foods, and we often cheer up children with chocolate. Therefore, a kitchen devoid of sugar can seem somewhat joyless, but you will discover that it is anything but.

There are both natural and chemical sugar alternatives that are easy to use and effective in baking. Stevia is a natural plant extract, and is grainy and exceptionally sweet, making it an excellent alternative to sugar. Rice malt syrup is made from fermented cooked brown rice and contains no fructose. With these two allies on hand, there are few baking challenges that cannot be overcome.

The best way to start with your sugar-free eating plan is by making your diet almost completely sugar-free to keep temptation at bay. Meats and cheeses can be enjoyed in moderation conscience-free, but choose carefully when buying processed products, such as bacon, ham, and smoked cheese, which can be made using sugar. The same goes for dairy products; flavored yogurts and creams are often loaded with sugar, so always read the label and, if necessary, go for a sugar-free alternative.

Another common source of processed sugar is refined carbohydrates, such as white flour and rice, and these should be avoided. Replace wheat flours with nut flours, ground almonds, coconut flour, and cornmeal. A number of the replacement flours contain some sugar, so use them in small quantities. Nuts and seeds are another splendid addition to your kitchen. They are great for texture and taste, and come in various forms, such as butters and flours. Snacking on unsalted nuts is a good way to diminish cravings and resist temptation.

Many vegetables are rich in carbohydrates and sugars. Leafy greens, from lettuce and spinach to kale and Swiss chard, are fine. Root vegetables can be more problematic; beets, parsnips, white potatoes, and carrots all contain high levels of sugar so should only be eaten in moderation. The sweet potato is acceptable in moderation, too, because it releases its sugar slowly into the bloodstream. The main family of veggies on your side are cruciferous vegetables, including cauliflower, cabbage, broccoli, and brussels sprouts. Most of these are bulky and full of vitamins and fiber.

Finally, berries are acceptable in moderation because they are relatively low in sugar. Blueberries, raspberries, strawberries, and cranberries are all packed with flavor and fiber.

BREAKFASTS

AVOCADO, BACON, AND CHILI FRITTATA

Inspired by the flavors of Mexico, this protein-packed frittata is wonderful lingered over on a lazy morning. You can make it ahead and store it in the refrigerator for up to two days.

SERVES: 4

PREP: 15 MINS COOK: 14 MINS

1 tablespoon vegetable oil
8 bacon strips, coarsely chopped
6 eggs, beaten
3 tablespoons heavy cream
2 large avocados, peeled and sliced
1 red chili, seeded and thinly sliced
1/2 lime
sea salt and pepper, to taste

1. Preheat the broiler to medium. Heat the oil in an 8-inch ovenproof skillet over medium heat. Add the bacon and cook, stirring, for 4–5 minutes, or until crisp and golden. Using a slotted spoon, transfer to a plate lined with paper towels. Remove the pan from the heat.

2. Pour the eggs into a bowl, add the cream, and season with salt and pepper, then beat. Return the pan to the heat. When it is hot, pour in the egg mixture and cook for 1–2 minutes, without stirring. Sprinkle the bacon and avocado on top and cook for an additional 2–3 minutes, or until the frittata is almost set and the underside is golden brown.

3. Place the frittata under the preheated broiler and cook for 3–4 minutes, or until the top is golden brown and the egg is set. Sprinkle with the chili and squeeze the lime juice over the top. Cut into wedges and serve.

COOKING BACON

The soft texture of the frittata works best with really crispy bacon. To achieve this, cook the bacon over medium heat until it has a dark golden color, then remove it from the pan and drain on paper towels.

PER SERVING: 525 CALS | 41.6G FAT | 15G SAT FAT | 8.8G CARBS | 1.5G SUGARS | 4.8G FIBER | 23.5G PROTEIN | 2.5G SALT

ZUCCHINI PANCAKES WITH SMOKED SALMON AND SCRAMBLED EGGS

Zucchini makes a beautiful substitute for potatoes in these tasty pancakes; their subtle creamy flavor complements the luxurious egg and salmon perfectly.

SERVES: 2
PREP: 30 MINS COOK: 18 MINS

3 extra-large eggs
1 tablespoon heavy cream
2 teaspoons finely snipped fresh chives
1 tablespoon butter
2 large slices of smoked salmon, to serve
sea salt and pepper, to taste

PANCAKES

1 large zucchini, grated
2 teaspoons quinoa flour
1/4 cup grated Parmesan cheese
1 extra-large egg yolk
1 tablespoon heavy cream
1 tablespoon vegetable oil

1. Preheat the oven to 225°F. To make the pancakes, lay a clean kitchen towel on a work surface and pile the zucchini in the center. Holding the kitchen towel over the sink, gather the sides together and twist them tightly until all the liquid from the zucchini has run out.

2. Put the zucchini, flour, Parmesan, egg yolk, and cream into a bowl and mix well. Roll the mixture into two balls and flatten them with the palms of your hands to make thick pancakes.

3. Heat the oil in a small skillet over medium–low heat. Cook the pancakes for 5–8 minutes on each side, or until golden brown. Remove from the heat, transfer to a baking sheet, and put them in the oven to keep warm.

4. To make the scrambled eggs, crack the eggs into a bowl, add the cream and chives, and season with salt and pepper. Beat with a fork until evenly mixed.

5. Wipe the skillet clean with paper towels, then melt the butter in the pan over low heat. Pour in the egg mixture and cook, stirring, for 5–6 minutes, or until the eggs are just set.

6. Put the warm pancakes on two plates. Spoon the scrambled eggs over them, then top with the salmon. Grind over some black pepper and serve immediately.

PERFECT SCRAMBLED EGGS

When cooking scrambled eggs, the trick any chef will tell you is "low and slow"—keep the heat down and stir patiently until the eggs start to bind. They will keep cooking all the time they're in the pan, so serve them quickly.

PER SERVING: 428 CALS | 33.2G FAT | 13.4G SAT FAT | 7.3G CARBS | 4G SUGARS | 1.6G FIBER | 25G PROTEIN | 2.2G SALT

MUSHROOMS ON RYE TOAST

This quick-and-easy breakfast is a real treat. If you can't find wild mushrooms, just increase the amount of cremini mushrooms instead. The rye bread is packed with fiber.

SERVES: 4
PREP: 8 MINS COOK: 8 MINS

3 tablespoons olive oil
2 large garlic cloves, crushed
3 cups sliced cremini mushrooms
3 cups sliced wild mushrooms
2 teaspoons lemon juice
2 tablespoons finely chopped fresh flat-leaf parsley
4 slices of rye bread
sea salt and pepper, to taste

1. Heat the oil in a large skillet over medium–low heat. Add the garlic and cook for a few seconds.
2. Increase the heat to high. Add the cremini mushrooms and cook, stirring continuously, for 3 minutes. Add the wild mushrooms and cook for an additional 2 minutes.
3. Stir in the lemon juice and parsley, and season with salt and pepper.
4. Lightly toast the rye bread, then transfer to a serving plate. Spoon the mushroom mixture over the toast and serve immediately.

MMM, MUSHROOMS

Darker mushrooms provide the antioxidant mineral selenium and are immune-boosting.

PER SERVING: 197 CALS | 11.3G FAT | 1.6G SAT FAT | 20.3G CARBS | 3.2G SUGARS | 2.5G FIBER | 5.5G PROTEIN | 1.3G SALT

EGGS FLORENTINE

This rich, classic dish is simple to prepare and perfect for a special occasion or a lazy weekend brunch.

SERVES: 4

PREP: 20 MINS COOK: 40 MINS

1 pound spinach leaves, trimmed and washed
4 tablespoons butter, plus extra to grease
1 cup sliced button mushrooms
1/3 cup pine nuts, toasted
6 scallions, thinly sliced
4 eggs
3 tablespoons whole-wheat flour
1 1/4 cups milk, warmed
1 teaspoon prepared English mustard
3/4 cup shredded sharp cheddar cheese
sea salt and pepper, to taste

1. Preheat the oven to 375°F. Lightly grease a shallow ovenproof dish with butter.

2. Drain the spinach well, then put it into a large saucepan. Place the pan over medium heat and sprinkle with a little salt. Cover and cook for 2–3 minutes, or until the spinach has wilted. Drain, pressing out any excess liquid, then chop and transfer to the prepared dish.

3. Melt 1 tablespoon of butter in a small saucepan over medium heat. Add the mushrooms and cook for 2 minutes, stirring often. Add the pine nuts and scallions and cook for an additional 2 minutes. Remove from the heat, season with salt and pepper, and sprinkle the mixture over the spinach, then keep warm.

4. Meanwhile, heat a wide, shallow saucepan of water until it is simmering but not at a rolling boil. Crack one egg into a cup, then stir the simmering water to make a whirlpool. As the whirlpool slows almost to a stop, gently slip the egg into its center. Cook for 2–3 minutes, or until set, then remove with a slotted spoon and place on top of the mushrooms. Repeat with the remaining three eggs.

5. Melt the remaining 3 tablespoons of butter in a saucepan over medium heat. Stir in the flour, then cook for 2 minutes. Remove from the heat and gradually stir in the milk. Return to the heat and cook, stirring constantly, until the mixture comes to a boil and has thickened. Add the mustard, then 1/2 cup of the cheese and stir until it has melted. Season with salt and pepper, then pour on top of the eggs, completely covering them. Sprinkle with the remaining cheese.

6. Bake for 20–25 minutes, or until piping hot and the top is golden brown and bubbling. Serve immediately.

SERVE IT WITH...

Chunky slices of spelt bread, plain or toasted, make a good accompaniment to this dish and soak up the tasty juices.

PER SERVING: 455 CALS | 35G FAT | 15G SAT FAT | 17.5G CARBS | 6G SUGARS | 4.5G FIBER | 22G PROTEIN | 1.6G SALT

COCONUT FLOUR PANCAKES WITH LEMON

Pancakes are the ultimate breakfast treat, and this version, made with coconut flour, really hits the spot. Pile them up and pour over some homemade lemon drizzle.

SERVES: 4

PREP: 15 MINS COOK: 10 MINS

2 extra-large eggs
1/2 cup coconut milk
4 cups cold water
1 teaspoon vanilla extract
1 tablespoon stevia
1/2 cup coconut flour
1 teaspoon baking soda
pinch of sea salt
1 tablespoon coconut oil
1/3 cup crème fraîche or Greek yogurt, to serve (optional)

LEMON DRIZZLE

finely grated zest and juice of 1 unwaxed lemon
2 teaspoons rice malt syrup

1. Crack the eggs into a bowl, then add the coconut milk, water, vanilla, stevia, flour, and baking soda and season with a pinch of sea salt. Whisk to a smooth batter, then let rest for a moment.

2. Meanwhile, to make the lemon drizzle, put the lemon zest and juice and rice malt syrup in a small bowl and mix well.

3. Heat the coconut oil in a large skillet over medium heat. Pour in a tablespoon of the batter, let settle for a moment, then add more tablespoons, allowing a little space between each one. Cook for 2 minutes, or until the bottom of each pancake is light brown and the sides are set. Carefully flip over the pancakes, using a spatula, and cook for an additional 2 minutes.

4. Transfer the pancakes to warm serving plates. Cook the remaining pancakes in the same way. Top each plate of pancakes with a tablespoon of crème fraîche or yogurt, if using, and spoon the lemon drizzle over the top.

GRATING LEMON ZEST

It is best to grate a lemon with a fine microplane, so you can ensure you take off just the zest and not the bitter white pith.

PER SERVING: 157 CALS | 14G FAT | 10.3G SAT FAT | 4.7G CARBS | 1.6G SUGARS | 1.2G FIBER | 4.5G PROTEIN | 1.3G SALT

COFFEE AND PECAN MINI BREAKFAST MUFFINS

Sometimes you feel you need a sweet hit in the morning to get you through the first few hours of the day. These muffins provide that with none of the sugar highs and crashes.

MAKES: 9 MUFFINS
PREP: 25 MINS COOK: 20 MINS

1/2 cup coconut flour
1/4 teaspoon baking powder
1/2 teaspoon baking soda
1 tablespoon stevia
1/3 cup coarsely chopped pecans
pinch of sea salt

TOPPING
2/3 cup sour cream
1/3 cup vegetable oil
2 extra-large eggs, beaten
1/3 cup prepared espresso or strong instant coffee
1 teaspoon rice malt syrup

1. Preheat the oven to 325°F. Put nine mini muffin cups into a mini muffin pan.

2. Put the flour, baking powder, baking soda, stevia, 3 tablespoons of the pecans, and a small pinch of salt in a large bowl and mix well. Add the sour cream, oil, eggs, and 1/4 cup of the espresso, and stir until evenly mixed. Let stand for a moment, then spoon the batter into the muffin cups.

3. Bake for 20 minutes, or until well risen and the tops spring back when pressed with a fingertip. Let cool for 5 minutes, then transfer to a wire rack.

4. To make the topping, put the rice malt syrup and remaining 1 tablespoon of espresso in a bowl and mix. Spoon a small drizzle over each muffin. Sprinkle on the remaining pecans and serve warm, or store in an airtight container for up to two days.

RICE MALT SYRUP

Baking with rice malt syrup is similar to baking with sugar in terms of quantity and texture. However, be aware that it can burn quickly. If you are concerned, loosely place a sheet of parchment paper over the top of your baked goods to protect the exposed areas while allowing the rest to continue to bake.

PER MUFFIN: 170 CALS | 16.6G FAT | 3.2G SAT FAT | 1.6G CARBS | 1.1G SUGARS | 0.5G FIBER | 3.6G PROTEIN | 0.5G SALT

BLUEBERRY AND OAT BREAKFAST BARS

These are like a cross between a cookie and an oat bar with their moist explosion of blueberries, and they will give you an energetic start to the day.

MAKES: 12 BARS

PREP: 15 MINS COOK: 25 MINS

- 1 stick unsalted butter
- 1/2 cup quinoa flour
- 1 cup rolled oats
- pinch of sea salt
- 1/2 teaspoon freshly grated nutmeg
- 1 teaspoon ground cinnamon
- 1/2 teaspoon ground allspice
- 1/2 teaspoon baking powder
- 1/2 teaspoon baking soda
- 2 tablespoons rice malt syrup
- 1 extra-large egg, beaten
- 1/2 cup blueberries
- 1/3 cup coarsely chopped cranberries (optional)

1. Preheat the oven to 325°F. Line a 10 1/2 x 6 1/2-inch cake pan with parchment paper. Melt the butter in a small saucepan, then pour it into a large bowl.
2. Put all the remaining ingredients apart from the blueberries and cranberries in the bowl and mix to a chunky batter. Carefully stir in the blueberries and cranberries, if using.
3. Pour the batter into the prepared pan and spread it into an even layer, using the back of a spoon. Bake for 20–25 minutes, or until golden brown and set.
4. Transfer to a wire rack to cool. After 10 minutes, cut into 12 bars, then let cool completely. Serve or store in an airtight container for up to three days.

COOL CRANBERRIES

Cranberries are packed with vitamin C and fiber, and have a good array of phytonutrients. They are also quite high in sugar, so eat in moderation.

PER BAR: 141 CALS | 8.9G FAT | 5G SAT FAT | 12G CARBS | 0.6G SUGARS | 1.7G FIBER | 3.3G PROTEIN | 0.3G SALT

CREAMY OATMEAL WITH BLACKBERRIES

Oats are complex carbohydrates that provide slow-release energy to keep you sustained throughout the morning.

SERVES: 2
PREP: 5 MINS COOK: 8 MINS

1/2 cup rolled oats
small pinch of sea salt
2 1/2 cups cold water
1/4 cup heavy cream, plus extra to serve
1 tablespoon stevia
1 tablespoon pumpkin seeds
6 large blackberries, quartered

1. Put the oats and salt in a medium saucepan and pour the water over them. Bring to a boil, then reduce the heat to medium–low and simmer, stirring regularly, for 5–6 minutes, or until the oats are thick but have a dense pouring consistency.

2. Stir in the cream and stevia. Spoon the oatmeal into two bowls, top with the pumpkin seeds and blackberries, and serve immediately with a little extra cream for pouring over the top.

ALSO TRY THIS

The Scots have made oatmeal with just water for generations, so you can omit the cream if you prefer. It does, however, provide calcium.

PER SERVING: 268 CALS | 9G FAT | 2.9G SAT FAT | 38G CARBS | 1.5G SUGARS | 7.2G FIBER | 11G PROTEIN | 0.7G SALT

NUTTY GRANOLA MEDLEY

Granola makes an excellent start to the day, but a handful of this crunchy nut and seed mixture is equally delicious as a snack when you're on the go.

SERVES: 6

PREP: 10 MINS COOK: 15 MINS

1 cup rolled oats
2 tablespoons shredded coconut
3 tablespoons pumpkin seeds
3 tablespoons slivered almonds
3 tablespoons pecans
1/4 cup flaxseed
2 tablespoons almond flour
1 tablespoon stevia
1 teaspoon ground cinnamon
1/2 teaspoon ground ginger
pinch of sea salt
1/4 cup almond butter
5 tablespoons unsalted butter
2 tablespoons plain yogurt, to serve

1. Preheat the oven to 325°F. Put the oats, coconut, pumpkin seeds, slivered almonds, and pecans in a food processor and pulse briefly to break everything into small chunks. Transfer the mixture to a large bowl, add the flaxseed, almond flour, stevia, spices, and salt, then mix well.

2. Melt the butters together in a small saucepan, stirring. Pour them over the dry ingredients and stir.

3. Spread the mixture evenly in a large roasting pan. Bake for 15 minutes; it should release a toasty aroma and be a light golden brown when ready. Let cool completely.

4. Shake the pan to break up the ingredients into chunky crumbs, with some larger shards. Serve with a tablespoon of plain yogurt or store in an airtight jar for up to one week.

PROTEIN FOR ENERGY

The nuts and seeds in this granola are packed with protein and fiber—the ideal weekday breakfast to keep you going until lunch.

PER SERVING: 302 CALS | 24.5G FAT | 8.8G SAT FAT | 15.2G CARBS | 0.8G SUGARS | 4.3G FIBER | 7.3G PROTEIN | 0.7G SALT

GREEK YOGURT WITH ORANGE ZEST AND TOASTED SEEDS

Toasting the seeds in this recipe enhances their flavor, so they contrast wonderfully with the smooth, creamy yogurt.

SERVES: 2

PREP: 5 MINS COOK: 3 MINS

2 teaspoons flaxseed
2 teaspoons pumpkin seeds
2 teaspoons chia seeds
1 cup plain Greek yogurt
grated zest of 1 small orange, plus 1 teaspoon juice

1. Place a small skillet over medium heat. When it is hot, add the seeds. Toast, stirring constantly with a wooden spoon, until they start to turn brown and release a nutty aroma. Transfer them to a plate and let cool.

2. Spoon the yogurt into two glass jars or serving bowls, then sprinkle the seeds on top, followed by the orange zest. Sprinkle with the orange juice and serve immediately.

FLAXSEED FOR HEALTH

Flaxseed are high in omega-3s, which are essential fatty acids that some studies show can help reduce the risk of heart disease and stroke.

PER SERVING: 172 CALS | 10.6G FAT | 4.3G SAT FAT | 8.1G CARBS | 4.3G SUGARS | 3.3G FIBER | 12G PROTEIN | TRACE SALT

RED PEPPER PEP-UP JUICE

Full of disease-fighting, anti-aging antioxidants, this juice provides loads of energy to help you get through the day.

SERVES: 2
PREP: 5 MINS

2 fennel bulbs with leaves, halved
1 apple, halved
1 small red bell pepper, halved
1 carrot, halved
1 cup cold water

1. Remove a few leaves from the fennel and reserve.
2. Feed the apple, followed by the fennel and bell pepper, then the carrot through a juicer.
3. Pour into a jug, add the water, and mix well.
4. Pour into two glasses, garnish with the reserved fennel leaves, and serve immediately.

AMAZING APPLES

Apples are a good source of vitamin C, soluble pectin (which is thought to help lower cholesterol), and the minerals calcium, magnesium, and phosphorus.

PER SERVING: 93 CALS | 0.5G FAT | TRACE SAT FAT | 21.9G CARBS | 10.9G SUGARS | 1.5G FIBER | 2.6G PROTEIN | 0.2G SALT

LUNCHES AND SNACKS

BEEF AND HERB SOUP

Forget store-bought soups, which often contain hidden sugars—this substantial homemade soup will keep you full for hours!

SERVES: 6
PREP: 20 MINS COOK: 1 HOUR

2 onions
2 tablespoons sunflower oil
1 tablespoon ground turmeric
1 teaspoon ground cumin
1/2 cup green or yellow split peas
5 cups beef stock
8 ounces ground beef
1 cup long-grain rice
1 tablespoon coarsely chopped fresh cilantro, plus extra to garnish
1 tablespoon finely snipped fresh chives
1 cup finely chopped baby spinach
2 tablespoons butter
2 garlic cloves, finely chopped
3 tablespoons coarsely chopped fresh mint
sea salt and pepper, to taste
1/3 cup plain Greek yogurt, to serve

1. Grate one of the onions into a large bowl and finely chop the other. Heat the oil in a large saucepan over medium-low heat. Add the chopped onion and cook, stirring occasionally, for 8–10 minutes, or until golden. Stir in the turmeric and cumin, add the split peas, and pour in the stock. Bring to a boil, then reduce the heat to low, cover, and simmer for 15 minutes.

2. Meanwhile, add the beef to the grated onion, season with salt and pepper, and mix. Shape the mixture into small balls.

3. Add the meatballs to the soup, replace the lid on the pan, and simmer for 10 minutes. Add the rice and stir in the cilantro, chives, and spinach. Simmer, stirring frequently, for 25–30 minutes, or until the rice is tender.

4. Melt the butter in a skillet over low heat. Add the garlic and cook, stirring frequently, for 2–3 minutes. Stir in the mint and cook for an additional minute.

5. Transfer the soup to bowls and sprinkle with the garlic mixture. Add a spoonful of yogurt to each bowl and sprinkle with the remaining cilantro.

SPLIT PEAS

Brimming with soluble fiber, split peas also contain loads of protein and two B vitamins. They are an inexpensive nutrient powerhouse.

PER SERVING: 344 CALS | 12.7G FAT | 5G SAT FAT | 40.8G CARBS | 3.9G SUGARS | 6.3G FIBER | 17G PROTEIN | 2.4G SALT

SWEET POTATO SOUP

This thick, colorful, and filling soup has a wonderful sweet flavor, yet the sugar levels are low.

SERVES: 6

PREP: 25 MINS   COOK: 30 MINS

1 tablespoon vegetable oil
1 onion, finely chopped
1-inch piece fresh ginger, peeled and finely chopped
1 teaspoon medium curry powder
1 teaspoon sea salt
3 sweet potatoes, coarsely chopped
$1^2/_3$ cups coconut milk
$3^3/_4$ cups vegetable stock
juice of 1 lime
2 tablespoons coarsely chopped fresh cilantro, to garnish

1. Heat the oil in a large, heavy saucepan over medium–high heat. Add the onion and ginger and cook, stirring, for 5 minutes, or until soft. Add the curry powder and salt and cook, stirring, for an additional minute. Add the sweet potatoes, coconut milk, and stock, then bring to a boil. Reduce the heat to medium and simmer, uncovered, for 20 minutes, or until the sweet potatoes are soft.

2. Puree the soup, either in batches in a blender or food processor, or using a handheld immersion blender. Return the soup to the heat, bring back up to a simmer, then stir in the lime juice. Transfer the soup to bowls and sprinkle with the cilantro.

SWEET POTATOES

High in vitamin C, potassium, and beta-carotene (which the body converts to vitamin A), sweet potatoes make a healthy addition to any meal. They are also a source of manganese.

PER SERVING: 242 CALS | 13.3G FAT | 9.8G SAT FAT | 27G CARBS | 7.2G SUGARS | 3.8G FIBER | 3G PROTEIN | 1.6G SALT

CLAMS IN BACON, LEEK, AND CREAM BROTH

Leeks pack plenty of flavor and are low in sugar. The bacon really complements the clams in this recipe.

SERVES: 4
PREP: 45 MINS   COOK: 1 HOUR

- 3½ pounds fresh live clams, scrubbed
- 1 teaspoon butter
- 12 bacon strips, coarsely chopped
- 2 leeks, sliced
- 1 garlic clove, finely chopped
- ½ cup brandy
- 1¼ cups cold water
- ½ cup light cream
- ¼ cup finely chopped fresh flat-leaf parsley

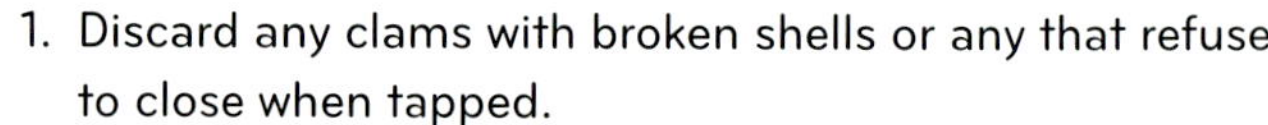

1. Discard any clams with broken shells or any that refuse to close when tapped.
2. Melt the butter in a deep, heavy saucepan over medium heat. Add the bacon and fry, stirring, for 4–5 minutes, or until crisp and golden. Using a slotted spoon, transfer to a plate lined with paper towels.
3. Put the leeks and garlic in the pan and cook, stirring regularly, for 5 minutes, or until softened but not browned.
4. Pour in the brandy and let simmer for a minute to burn off the alcohol (brandy in a hot pan can easily flame, so be careful). Add the water and stir well. Turn up the heat to medium-high and, when the water starts to boil, toss in the clams. Put on the lid and steam for 5 minutes, or until the clams have opened.
5. Take the pan off the heat. Discard any clams that remain closed. Stir in the bacon and cream. Sprinkle with the parsley and serve in bowls, with a large empty bowl to collect the shells.

BUYING BACON

Try to find a brand of bacon that has no sugar content in the cure.

PER SERVING: 380 CALS | 20.5G FAT | 9.6G SAT FAT | 9.8G CARBS | 3G SUGARS | 0.9G FIBER | 25G PROTEIN | 2.2G SALT

WARM QUINOA, ROASTED SQUASH, AND PINE NUT SALAD

Quinoa is considered a sacred food by the Incas, and has long been prized for its flavor and ability to keep you feeling full. Loaded with protein and vitamins, it is perfect for a salad.

SERVES: 2

PREP: 20 MINS COOK: 30 MINS

1/2 cup white quinoa, rinsed
1 1/2 cups cold water
1 1/2 cups peeled and seeded acorn squash, butternut squash, or pumpkin chunks
1/4 cup olive oil
pinch of cayenne pepper
2 tablespoons pine nuts
1/4 cup coarsely chopped fresh flat-leaf parsley
3/4 cup baby spinach
juice of 1/4 lemon, plus lemon wedges to serve
sea salt and pepper, to taste

1. Preheat the oven to 350°F. Put the quinoa in a saucepan. Add the water, bring to a boil, then cover and simmer over low heat for 10 minutes. Remove from the heat, but leave the pan covered for an additional 7 minutes to let the grains swell. Fluff up with a fork.

2. Meanwhile, put the squash and 2 tablespoons of oil in a large roasting pan, sprinkle with the cayenne and a pinch of salt, and toss well. Roast for 25 minutes, or until crisp on the edges and tender. Transfer to a large bowl.

3. Toast the pine nuts in a dry skillet over high heat until they are light brown, then transfer to the bowl. Gently mix in the quinoa, parsley, and spinach, being careful that nothing breaks up, then season with salt and pepper.

4. Divide the salad between two plates, drizzle with the remaining oil and the lemon juice, and serve with lemon wedges for squeezing over the salad.

COOKING QUINOA

Cooked quinoa should have a texture similar to slightly chewy couscous, but be careful not to overcook it. If the pan boils dry during cooking, add a splash more water and turn off the heat, then let rest for 10 minutes with the lid on; the trapped steam should be enough to finish cooking the quinoa without saturating it.

PER SERVING: 521 CALS | 37G FAT | 4.5G SAT FAT | 40.5G CARBS | 2G SUGARS | 4.6G FIBER | 9.9G PROTEIN | 1.5G SALT

GREEK SALAD CROSTINI

Crisp, toasted high-fiber country-style bread is topped with a classic salad packed with vibrant Mediterranean flavors.

SERVES: 4

PREP: 20 MINS COOK: 5 MINS

- 1 garlic clove, crushed
- 1/4 cup olive oil
- 2 slices of seeded whole-wheat bread
- 7 ounces feta cheese, diced
- 1/4 cucumber, finely diced
- 1/4 cup sliced, pitted black ripe olives
- 4 plum tomatoes, coarsely chopped
- 1/4 small onion, coarsely chopped
- 2 tablespoons fresh mint leaves, shredded
- 2 sprigs fresh oregano, chopped
- 1 lettuce heart, finely shredded
- 1/2 teaspoon toasted sesame seeds
- 2 teaspoons pine nuts (optional)
- pepper, to taste

1. Preheat the broiler to medium-high. Put the garlic and oil in a large bowl and mix well.

2. Put the bread on the broiler rack, brush lightly with some of the garlic oil, and toast well away from the heat for 2–3 minutes, or until crisp and golden. Turn the bread and brush lightly with more oil, then toast again.

3. Add the feta cheese to the remaining garlic oil in the bowl and season with pepper. Mix in the cucumber, olives, tomatoes, onion, mint, and oregano, then gently mix in the lettuce.

4. Spoon the salad and its juices over the toast. Sprinkle with the sesame seeds and pine nuts, if using. Cut each piece of toast in half and serve half per person.

SESAME SEEDS

Sesame seeds are packed with minerals, vitamins, and antioxidants. They are especially rich in monounsaturated fatty acids, which are considered to help prevent heart disease and stroke.

PER SERVING: 379 CALS | 28.8G FAT | 9.7G SAT FAT | 20.2G CARBS | 6.7G SUGARS | 3.6G FIBER | 11.5G PROTEIN | 2.8G SALT

FLATBREAD PIZZAS WITH GARLIC ZUCCHINI RIBBONS

This fresh, Mediterranean-style lunch with a satisfying crunchy crust and fresh vegetable topping is sure to keep hunger pangs at bay.

SERVES: 2
PREP: 20 MINS COOK: 10 MINS

1/4 cup crème fraîche (or extra ricotta cheese)
1 zucchini, shredded into ribbons using a vegetable peeler
4 cherry tomatoes, quartered
1/4 cup ricotta cheese
1 garlic clove, crushed
2 tablespoons olive oil
salad greens, to serve (optional)

PIZZA CRUSTS

3/4 cup whole-wheat flour, plus extra to dust
1/3 cup quinoa flour
3/4 teaspoon baking soda
1 tablespoon olive oil
2 tablespoons warm water
sea salt, to taste

KNEADING DOUGH

Push the dough down, stretching it out in front of you, using the heels of your hands. You are trying to stretch the gluten strands in it. Fold the top half of the dough back toward you and press down and stretch again. Continue like this until the dough is smooth and elastic.

1. Preheat the oven to 400°F. To make the pizza crusts, put the flours and baking soda in a mixing bowl, season with salt, and stir. Add the oil, then gradually mix in enough of the warm water to make a soft but not sticky dough.

2. Lightly dust a work surface with flour. Knead the dough on the surface for 2 minutes, or until smooth and slightly elastic.

3. Put two large, flat baking sheets in the oven to get hot.

4. Divide the dough into two pieces. Roll out each piece to a circle about 1/4 inch thick. Remove the hot baking sheets from the oven and, working quickly, lay the dough on top. Spread the crème fraîche over the pizza crusts, then sprinkle with the zucchini and tomatoes. Blob the ricotta cheese in small dollops on top and put the pizzas in the oven.

5. Bake for 7–10 minutes, or until the crust is crispy and slightly puffed up, and the ricotta is tinged golden.

6. Mix the garlic and oil together in a small bowl, then drizzle it over the hot pizzas. Serve with salad greens, if using.

PER SERVING: 568 CALS | 31.4G FAT | 8G SAT FAT | 57.6G CARBS | 3.7G SUGARS | 8.2G FIBER | 14G PROTEIN | 2.1G SALT

ASPARAGUS WITH HOT-SMOKED SALMON AND POACHED EGG

Asparagus, salmon, and poached eggs with lemony butter make a luxurious lunch or summer appetizer.

SERVES: 2
PREP: 25 MINS COOK: 21 MINS

- 4 tablespoons unsalted butter, softened
- finely grated zest of 1/2 unwaxed lemon, plus 1/2 teaspoon juice
- sprig of fresh dill, coarsely chopped
- 14 ounces hot-smoked salmon
- 10 asparagus spears, woody stems removed
- 2 extra-large eggs
- sea salt and pepper, to taste

1. Preheat the oven to 350°F. Put the butter, lemon zest and juice, and dill in a small bowl, season with salt and pepper, and mix. Pat the butter into an approximate square with the back of a spoon, wrap it in plastic wrap, and chill in the refrigerator while you make the rest of the dish.
2. Wrap the hot-smoked salmon in aluminum foil and bake for 15 minutes. Flake the fish into bite-size pieces and keep warm.
3. Cook the asparagus in a saucepan of lightly salted boiling water for 2 minutes. Drain and hold under cold running water briefly to stop the cooking process, then set aside.
4. Heat a second wide saucepan of water until it is almost at simmering point. Crack one egg into a cup, then stir the water to make a whirlpool. As the whirlpool slows almost to a stop, gently slip the egg into its center. Cook for 2–3 minutes, then remove with a slotted spoon. Repeat with the second egg.
5. Put five asparagus spears on each of two plates, top with half the flaked salmon, then balance a poached egg on top and crown with a pat of lemon butter. The remaining heat from the egg should melt the butter into a scrumptious lemon herb sauce. Serve immediately.

ALSO TRY THIS

If you don't like lemon, replace it with parsley and a little crushed garlic.

PER SERVING: 618 CALS | 40G FAT | 18.6G SAT FAT | 3.5G CARBS | 1.7G SUGARS | 1.7G FIBER | 58G PROTEIN | 2.5G SALT

NO-CRUST SQUASH, CHORIZO, AND GOAT CHEESE QUICHE

This simple quiche is brimming with energy-boosting chorizo and vitamin-packed butternut squash—and is ideal for packing into a lunch bag.

SERVES: 4

PREP: 30 MINS CHILL: 30 MINS COOK: 1 HOUR 20 MINS

1 butternut squash, peeled, seeded, and diced
1 tablespoon olive oil
7 ounces chorizo, cut into small, irregular chunks
3 eggs
1/2 cup crème fraîche or sour cream
2 tablespoons fresh thyme leaves
4 ounces semihard goat cheese
sea salt and pepper, to taste
salad greens, to serve (optional)

PASTRY DOUGH

4 tablespoons cold butter, diced
3/4 cup whole-wheat flour, plus extra to dust
2 tablespoons cold water

1. Preheat the oven to 375°F. To make the dough, put the butter in a mixing bowl, add the flour, and season with salt and pepper. Rub the butter into the flour until it resembles fine bread crumbs. Alternatively, process it in a food processor. Gradually mix in enough water to make a soft but not sticky dough.

2. Lightly dust a work surface with flour. Pat the dough into a disk (see "Chilling Dough" to the right), then wrap it in plastic wrap. Chill in the refrigerator for at least 30 minutes.

CHILLING DOUGH

Just before you put the wrapped pastry in the refrigerator, shape it into a flat-topped disk—like a big burger patty. This will make it easier to roll.

3. Meanwhile, to make the filling, put the butternut squash and oil in a large roasting pan, season with salt and pepper, and toss well. Roast for 15 minutes, then stir and add the chorizo. Roast for an additional 15 minutes, or until the squash is crisp on the edges and tender, and the chorizo is crisp. Set aside to cool.

4. Dust the work surface with more flour. Knead the dough gently, then roll it out to a circle just under 9 inches in diameter. Place on a baking sheet and prick all over with a fork. Bake for 20 minutes. Remove from the oven and, using the bottom of an 8-inch loose-bottom tart pan as a template, cut a circle in the pastry. Set aside to cool.

5. Meanwhile, crack the eggs into a large bowl and lightly beat with a fork. Stir in the crème fraîche or sour cream and thyme and season with plenty of pepper.

6. Line the 8-inch tart pan with parchment paper. Carefully place your cooled pastry circle in the pan, then sprinkle with the chorizo and butternut squash. Pour the egg mixture over them, then crumble the goat cheese on top. Reduce the oven temperature to 325°F. Bake the quiche for 30 minutes, or until the egg in the center is set. Serve warm or cold, with salad greens, if using.

PER SERVING: 677 CALS | 49.7G FAT | 23.5G SAT FAT | 32G CARBS | 3.9G SUGARS | 4.7G FIBER | 27.5G PROTEIN | 3G SALT

BLUE CHEESE AND HERB PÂTÉ

An easy-to-make light lunch, this filling pâté is also ideal for an appetizer or for packing in a summer picnic.

SERVES: 4

PREP: 20 MINS CHILL: 30 MINS COOK: 1 MIN

- 2/3 cup cream cheese
- 1 1/2 cups fromage blanc or ricotta cheese
- 4 ounces blue cheese, crumbled
- 2 tablespoons finely chopped dried cranberries
- 1/4–1/2 cup finely chopped fresh herbs, such as flat-leaf parsley, chives, dill, and tarragon
- 6 tablespoons butter
- 3 tablespoons coarsely chopped walnuts
- 4 slices of whole-grain bread, to serve

1. Put the cream cheese into a bowl and beat well with a metal spoon to soften. Gradually beat in the fromage blanc or ricotta cheese until smooth. Add the blue cheese, cranberries, and herbs, and stir well. Spoon the mixture into four ramekins or other small dishes and smooth the tops.

2. Melt the butter in a small saucepan over low heat. Skim any foam off the surface and discard it. Carefully pour the clear yellow layer into a small bowl, leaving the milky liquid in the pan. The yellow layer is the clarified butter; discard the remaining liquid in the pan.

3. Pour a little of the clarified butter over each ramekin of pâté and sprinkle with the walnuts. Cover with plastic wrap and chill in the refrigerator for at least 30 minutes, or until firm.

4. Toast the bread and serve the pâté alongside it, spreading some onto the toast.

SLOW-RELEASE ENERGY

Protein from the cheese provides the slow-release energy you need to keep going without feeling the need to top up with sugar.

PER SERVING: 455 CALS | 40G FAT | 24G SAT FAT | 9.8G CARBS | 7.8G SUGARS | 0.5G FIBER | 15.5G PROTEIN | 1.8G SALT

SMOKY PAPRIKA SWEET POTATO FRIES WITH SOUR CREAM DIP

Starchy and sweet, with crunchy edges and fluffy insides, these fries make a really satisfying snack. Always use the best paprika you can find.

SERVES: 2

PREP: 10 MINS   COOK: 40 MINS

2 sweet potatoes, unpeeled, scrubbed, and cut into sticks or wedges
2 tablespoons olive oil
1 tablespoon smoked paprika
sea salt and pepper, to taste

SOUR CREAM DIP

4 chives, finely snipped
2/3 cup sour cream

1. Preheat the oven to 350°F. Put the sweet potatoes, oil, and smoked paprika in a large bowl, season with salt and pepper, and toss well.

2. Arrange the sweet potatoes in a single layer on a large baking sheet. Bake for 30–40 minutes, or until crisp.

3. To make the dip, put the chives and sour cream in a bowl and mix. Season with salt and pepper and divide between two small dipping bowls.

4. Line two larger bowls with paper towels. Transfer the fries to the bowls and serve immediately with the dip.

ALSO TRY THIS

This dip works well with 2 tablespoons of finely chopped fresh flat-leaf parsley instead of chives, or try mixing in 1/2 teaspoon of smoked paprika.

PER SERVING: 399 CALS | 28.4G FAT | 10.4G SAT FAT | 32.8G CARBS | 8.8G SUGARS | 5G FIBER | 4G PROTEIN | 1.1G SALT

CRUNCHY PARMESAN AND KALE CHIPS

This recipe for kale chips will be one of the simplest dishes you'll ever make. They're deliciously crisp, with a salty kick from the Parmesan.

SERVES: 4
PREP: 10 MINS COOK: 15 MINS

7 ounces kale, woody stems removed
1 tablespoon olive oil
pinch of cayenne pepper
1 cup finely grated Parmesan cheese
sea salt, to taste

1. Preheat the oven to 350°F. Put the kale and oil in a bowl, season with the cayenne pepper and salt, then toss.

2. Arrange the kale in a single layer on a large baking sheet. Sprinkle the cheese over the kale. Bake for 10–15 minutes, or until the leaves are dry and crisp but just a little brown at the edges.

3. Let cool for 5 minutes, until crisp, then serve.

BAKING KALE

Watch your kale very closely; if it overcooks and the leaves turn brown, they will be bitter.

PER SERVING: 153 CALS | 10.2G FAT | 4.6G SAT FAT | 5.8G CARBS | 0.2G SUGARS | 1G FIBER | 10.6G PROTEIN | 1.4G SALT

CHOCOLATE AND BRAZIL NUT BARS

These bars are ideal for anyone with a sweet tooth. They have a crunchy, chewy texture and are perfect for when you're out and about.

MAKES: 9 BARS
PREP: 20 MINS COOK: 4 MINS CHILL: 30 MINS

1 cup slivered almonds
8 Brazil nuts, coarsely chopped
5 tablespoons unsalted butter
1/4 cup almond butter
1 teaspoon vanilla extract
pinch of sea salt
1/2 cup ground almonds (almond meal)
1/2 cup shredded dry coconut
1 1/2 tablespoons rice malt syrup
2 teaspoons unsweetened cocoa powder
3/4 ounce bittersweet chocolate, cut into small chunks

1. Line a 8-inch square cake pan with parchment paper. Toast the slivered almonds and Brazil nuts in a dry skillet over high heat until they are light brown, then transfer them to a large mixing bowl.

2. Melt the butters together in a small saucepan over low heat. Stir in the vanilla and a pinch of salt.

3. Add all the remaining ingredients to the toasted nuts, then stir. Add the melted butter mixture and stir again. Transfer the mixture to the prepared pan and, using the back of a spoon, spread it out to reach all the corners. Cover and chill in the refrigerator for 30 minutes, or until set.

4. Cut into nine bars and wrap each in parchment paper. Store in an airtight container in the refrigerator for up to two days.

SAVE TIME

Pulse the Brazil nuts momentarily in a food processor to chop them. If you buy whole instead of slivered almonds, they can be chopped in this way, too.

PER BAR: 334 CALS | 31.5G FAT | 9.6G SAT FAT | 9.9G CARBS | 3G SUGARS | 4.1G FIBER | 7.8G PROTEIN | 0.2G SALT

DARK CHOCOLATE AND PEANUT BUTTER ENERGY BALLS

Bittersweet chocolate that is low in added sugar and high in cocoa is one of the star ingredients of the low-sugar kitchen if used in small amounts.

MAKES: 8 BALLS
PREP: 15 MINS CHILL: 30 MINS

$^1/_3$ cup almond flour
$^1/_4$ cup unsweetened peanut butter
3 tablespoons coarsely chopped unsalted peanuts
3 tablespoons flaxseed
1 ounce bittersweet chocolate, finely chopped
1 teaspoon unsweetened cocoa powder
pinch of sea salt

1. Put the almond flour in a food processor and process for a minute, until you have the texture of coarse flour.

2. Put the peanut butter, peanuts, flaxseed, chocolate, and a small pinch of salt into a bowl and mix. Add the almond flour, reserving $1^1/_2$ tablespoons. Mix until you have a texture resembling chunky clay.

3. Sprinkle the remaining almond flour and the cocoa powder onto a plate and mix with a teaspoon. Form a tablespoon-size blob of the peanut mixture into a ball, using your palms. Roll it in the cocoa powder mixture, then transfer to a plate. Make an additional seven balls in the same way.

4. Cover and chill in the refrigerator for at least 30 minutes, or up to two days.

ALSO TRY THIS

If the coating of cocoa powder is too bitter and strong for your taste, substitute it with a teaspoon of ground cinnamon.

PER BALL: 144 CALS | 11.9G FAT | 2.1G SAT FAT | 5.9G CARBS | 1.7G SUGARS | 3G FIBER | 4.9G PROTEIN | 0.3G SALT

GINGER AND OAT NO-BAKE COOKIES

This is a low-sugar version of oat bars. Sweet, gingery, and oaty, it has an irresistible flavor and plenty of texture.

MAKES: 8 COOKIES

PREP: 10 MINS COOK: 8 MINS CHILL: 25 MINS

4 tablespoons unsalted butter
1 cup heavy cream
$1^1/_2$ tablespoon unsweetened smooth peanut butter
3 tablespoons rice malt syrup
1 tablespoon ground ginger
2 cups rolled oats

1. Put the butter, cream, and peanut butter into a saucepan and bring to a boil over medium heat, stirring from time to time. Turn the heat down to medium-low and cook for 5 minutes.

2. Add all the remaining ingredients to the pan and stir.

3. Line a baking sheet with parchment paper. Drop tablespoons of the dough onto the sheet—it should make eight cookies—then cover and chill in the refrigerator for 25 minutes before serving.

ALSO TRY THIS

If you're not a fan of ginger, try using the same amount of ground cinnamon or allspice instead.

PER COOKIE: 175 CALS | 11.8G FAT | 6.3G SAT FAT | 14G CARBS | 1.6G SUGARS | 2G FIBER | 3.8G PROTEIN | 0.2G SALT

MAIN DISHES

RIB EYE STEAK, CHIMICHURRI SAUCE, AND MASHED SWEET POTATOES

Chimichurri is an Argentinian herb sauce with a texture similar to coarse pesto. Most regions have a variation on it, such as adding anchovies or removing the chili.

SERVES: 2

PREP: 30 MINS COOK: 22 MINS

1 tablespoon olive oil
2 rib eye steaks, 4½ ounces each
½ teaspoon ground cumin
sea salt and pepper, to taste

CHIMICHURRI SAUCE

¼ cup fresh flat-leaf parsley, coarsely chopped
1 tablespoon fresh oregano
3 small garlic cloves, coarsely chopped
½ shallot, coarsely chopped
¼ red chili, seeded and coarsely chopped
3 tablespoons extra-virgin olive oil
1 teaspoon red wine vinegar
juice of ¼ lemon

MASHED SWEET POTATOES

2 small sweet potatoes, cut into ¾-inch chunks
1½ tablespoons butter

1. To make the mashed sweet potatoes, cook the sweet potatoes in a large saucepan of lightly salted boiling water for 12–15 minutes, or until soft. Drain, then allow to steam dry in the pan off the heat for at least 5 minutes. Using a potato masher, mash the potatoes to a smooth consistency.

2. Meanwhile, to make the chimichurri sauce, put all the ingredients in a food processor, season with salt and pepper, and process until you have a paste of a similar consistency to pesto. Add a little extra olive oil if the mixture appears too thick. Spoon into a serving bowl, cover, and set aside.

3. Return the mash to the heat and warm through before stirring in the butter. Season with salt and pepper, and keep warm.

4. Massage the oil into both sides of each steak, then sprinkle with salt and the cumin. Heat a flat ridged grill pan over high heat until smoking hot. Cook each steak for 2–3 minutes on each side, or for longer if you prefer it well done. Let the steaks rest for 2 minutes.

5. Serve a steak on each of two plates with the chimichurri sauce spooned over them and the mashed sweet potatoes on the side.

STEAK POWER

Steak is crammed with selenium and zinc and contains moderate amounts of iron and phosphorus. It is also a good source of protein and the B vitamins.

PER SERVING: 691 CALS | 52.8G FAT | 15.7G SAT FAT | 26.4G CARBS | 5.2G SUGARS | 3.8G FIBER | 27G PROTEIN | 2G SALT

STEAK, BROCCOLI, AND SESAME SEED STIR-FRY

Vibrant green broccoli and juicy beef are the stars of this stir-fry, and the sesame oil introduces a nutty depth and richness.

SERVES: 2

PREP: 15 MINS PLUS MARINATING COOK: 10 MINS

1 tablespoon soy sauce, plus extra to serve
1 tablespoon sesame oil, plus extra to serve
7-ounce tenderloin steak, cut into strips
2 teaspoons sesame seeds
1 tablespoon peanut oil
1 large garlic clove, thinly sliced
1/2 red chili, seeded and thinly sliced lengthwise (optional)
9 ounces baby broccoli
3 tablespoons water

1. Mix the soy sauce and sesame oil in a large bowl, add the steak, and toss. Cover and leave to marinate for 10 minutes.

2. Toast the sesame seeds in a large, dry wok over high heat until they are just beginning to brown, then tip them into the bowl with the steak and set aside.

3. Remove the wok from the heat and wipe it clean with paper towels. Return to the heat and pour in the oil. Remove the steak from the marinade and quickly cook it, turning from time to time, until browned on all sides and cooked to your liking. Transfer it to a plate and set aside.

4. If the pan is dry, add a splash more oil, then sauté the garlic and chili, if using. Add the broccoli, steak marinade, and water, stir, and cook for 1 minute, until the broccoli is bright green and just beginning to soften.

5. Return the steak to the wok and stir well. Divide the stir-fry between two plates and drizzle with extra soy sauce and sesame oil. Serve immediately.

ALSO TRY THIS

Add a 1-inch piece of fresh ginger, finely grated, with the garlic and chili in step four and stir in a handful of finely chopped fresh cilantro at the end of step five.

PER SERVING: 366 CALS | 24.5G FAT | 4.8G SAT FAT | 10.5G CARBS | 2.2G SUGARS | 4.1G FIBER | 28.6G PROTEIN | 1.4G SALT

HEARTY BEEF STEW WITH HERBED CHEESE DUMPLINGS AND KALE

Rich, deep, and comforting, this delicious winter stew will draw everyone to the table and fill the hungriest of diners.

SERVES: 4

PREP: 30 MINS COOK: 3 HOURS

- 1/4 cup olive oil
- 1/2 onion, finely chopped
- 1 leek, thinly sliced
- 1 celery stalk, coarsely chopped
- 4 garlic cloves, finely chopped
- 1 teaspoon tomato paste
- 2 pounds beef shank, cut into bite-size chunks
- 1/3 cup quinoa flour
- 1/2 cup brandy
- 3 1/2 cups beef stock
- 1 tablespoon fresh thyme leaves
- 2 tablespoons finely chopped fresh flat-leaf parsley
- 2 teaspoons smoked paprika
- 6 cloves
- 2 fresh bay leaves
- sea salt and pepper, to taste
- 7 ounces kale, coarsely chopped, to serve
- juice of 1/4 lemon, to serve

DUMPLINGS

- 1 cup quinoa flour
- 2 tablespoons beef suet or lard
- 1/2 cup shredded sharp cheddar cheese
- 1 teaspoon baking powder
- 1 tablespoon fresh thyme leaves
- 2 tablespoons finely chopped fresh flat-leaf parsley
- 1/4 cup water

1. Heat 2 tablespoons of the oil in a large lidded casserole dish over medium heat. Add the onion, leek, and celery, and sauté for 5 minutes, or until softened. Add the garlic and tomato paste, stir well, then turn the heat down to medium-low and let simmer while you cook the meat.

2. Heat the remaining oil in a large, heavy skillet over high heat until smoking hot. Season the beef with salt and pepper, then add it to the pan, in batches, and cook for a few minutes, turning, until browned on all sides. Using a slotted spoon, transfer the first batch to a plate while you brown the rest of the meat. Toss the browned meat into the casserole dish, then stir in the quinoa flour.

3. Turn the heat down to medium-high. Deglaze the beef skillet with the brandy, being careful because it can flame. Scrape all the meaty goodness off the bottom of the pan into the bubbling brandy with a wooden spoon, then add to the casserole dish. Pour in the stock, then add the thyme, parsley, paprika, cloves, and bay leaves, and season with salt and pepper.

4. Bring to a light boil, then turn the heat down to low and put on the lid. Simmer for 2–2 1/2 hours, or until the sauce is thick and the meat is soft enough to pull apart with a spoon.

5. To make the dumplings, put the quinoa flour, suet, cheese, baking powder, thyme, and parsley into a large bowl and mix well. Add the water, a little at a time, mixing, until you have a firm dough. Shape the mixture into 12 small balls.

6. After 2–2 1/2 hours cooking, remove the lid from the stew and arrange the dumplings on top. Put the lid back on and cook for 20 minutes.

7. Cook the kale in a large saucepan of lightly salted boiling water for 2 minutes. Drain, then squeeze over the lemon juice and toss lightly. Serve immediately with the stew.

PER SERVING: 830 CALS | 39.7G FAT | 14.5G SAT FAT | 41G CARBS | 3G SUGARS | 5G FIBER | 60G PROTEIN | 3.9G SALT

ITALIAN MEAT SAUCE

A rich, filling, traditional Italian sauce that tastes delicious served stirred into whole-wheat tagliatelle.

SERVES: 4

PREP: 10 MINS COOK: 1 HOURS

1 ounce dried porcini
1/2 cup lukewarm water
1 tablespoon butter
2 ounces pancetta, diced
1 small onion, finely chopped
1 garlic clove, finely chopped
2 small carrots, finely chopped
2 celery stalks, finely chopped
10 1/2 ounces ground beef
pinch of freshly grated nutmeg
1 tablespoon tomato paste
1/2 cup red wine
1 cup tomato puree or sauce
2 tablespoons finely chopped fresh flat-leaf parsley
sea salt and pepper, to taste
1 pound fresh whole-wheat tagliatelle (optional)

1. Soak the porcini in the water for 20 minutes, then drain well, reserving the soaking water.

2. Meanwhile, melt the butter in a heavy saucepan over medium heat. Add the pancetta and sauté, stirring, for 4 minutes, or until cooked.

3. Add the onion and garlic and sauté for 4 minutes, or until translucent. Add the carrots and celery, and cook for an additional few minutes, stirring often.

4. Add the ground beef and cook, stirring constantly, for 5 minutes, or until browned. Season with salt and pepper and add the nutmeg. Stir in the tomato paste and cook for 1–2 minutes, then pour in the wine and tomato puree or sauce.

5. Thinly slice the porcini, then add them to the sauce. Pour in the soaking water through a fine strainer. Cook for 1 hour, or until you have a thickened sauce and the beef is cooked.

6. Meanwhile, cook the tagliatelle, if using, according to the package directions, then drain well. Sprinkle the sauce with the parsley and serve with the tagliatelle, if using.

CHOICE OF PASTA

Italians traditionally serve this Italian meat sauce with tagliatelle, not spaghetti.

PER SERVING: 272 CALS | 11G FAT | 5.1G SAT FAT | 14.6G CARBS | 5G SUGARS | 3G FIBER | 21G PROTEIN | 1.6G SALT

BLACK RICE RISOTTO WITH PROSCIUTTO AND CHARRED ENDIVE

Black rice (or "forbidden" rice) contains large amounts of antitoxins and fiber, as well as being low in sugar, and makes a change from traditional risotto rice.

SERVES: 4
PREP: 10 MINS COOK: 1 HOUR

1 cup black rice
6 prosciutto slices
1 tablespoon olive oil
2 small heads endive, quartered lengthwise
1 tablespoon butter
2 garlic cloves, thinly sliced
1 small shallot, coarsely chopped
2 cups chicken stock
2 tablespoons mascarpone cheese
2 tablespoons coarsely chopped fresh flat-leaf parsley
sea salt, to taste

1. Cook the rice in a large saucepan of lightly salted boiling water for 45 minutes, or according to the package directions, until tender but slightly chewy.

2. Heat a deep skillet over medium-high heat. Add the prosciutto and dry-fry for 30 seconds on each side, or until crisp. Transfer to a plate.

3. Add the oil to the pan, then fry the endive heads for 2 minutes on each side, or until darkly golden. Remove from the pan, wrap in aluminum foil to keep warm, and set aside.

4. Reduce the heat to medium, then melt the butter in the pan. Add the garlic and shallot and sauté for 4 minutes, or until softened. Add the cooked and drained rice and stock, bring to a simmer, then cook gently for 5 minutes, or until two-thirds of the liquid has been absorbed. Stir in the mascarpone and parsley, then return the endive heads to the pan and warm through.

5. Crumble the prosciutto into large shards. Serve the risotto piled into four bowls with the crisp prosciutto on top.

WHY EAT BLACK RICE?

Black rice is arguably even better for you than whole-grain rice because the bran hull contains significantly higher amounts of vitamin E, which boosts the immune system.

PER SERVING: 346 CALS | 17.6G FAT | 8.3G SAT FAT | 38G CARBS | 2.8G SUGARS | 2.9G FIBER | 12G PROTEIN | 2.8G SALT

FRIED CHICKEN WITH SPICY RED CABBAGE COLESLAW

Instead of the usual bread crumbs, this chicken has a really crunchy coating of cornmeal, quinoa flour, and whole-wheat flour, which works well with the zingy coleslaw.

SERVES: 4

PREP: 20 MINS PLUS MARINATING COOK: 35 MINS

1 cup sour cream
1/2 teaspoon cayenne pepper
1 garlic clove, crushed
4 chicken thighs and 4 chicken drumsticks (about 2 pounds)
2 teaspoons cornmeal
2 tablespoons quinoa flour
2 tablespoons whole-wheat flour
oil for deep frying
sea salt and pepper, to taste

COLESLAW

2 cups shredded red cabbage
1 fennel bulb, shredded
1 red chili, seeded and thinly sliced lengthwise
1/2 cup plain Greek yogurt
juice of 1/4 lemon

1. Put the sour cream, cayenne, and garlic in a large bowl and season well with salt and pepper. Add the chicken and toss well. Cover the bowl with plastic wrap and chill in the refrigerator for 2–3 hours, or overnight if you have time.

2. To make the coleslaw, put all the ingredients in a large bowl and toss well, then season with salt and pepper. Cover and chill in the refrigerator.

3. Mix together the cornmeal and flours on a plate and season with salt and pepper. Fill a heavy skillet halfway with oil and place it over medium-high heat. Heat the oil to 350°F, or until a cube of bread browns in 30 seconds. While it heats, sprinkle the flour mixture over the chicken.

4. Cook the chicken in two batches because too much chicken in the pan will make the oil temperature drop. Using tongs, carefully place half the chicken in the oil. Cook for 6–8 minutes, then turn and cook for an additional 6–8 minutes, until the coating is a deep golden brown, the chicken is cooked through to the bone, and the juices run clear with no sign of pink when the tip of a sharp knife is inserted into the thickest part of the meat.

5. Using a slotted spoon, transfer the cooked chicken to paper towels to drain, then keep warm in a low oven while you cook the second batch.

6. Serve the chicken on a sharing board with the coleslaw.

PER SERVING: 695 CALS | 47.4G FAT | 14.5G SAT FAT | 30G CARBS | 6G SUGARS | 6G FIBER | 38G PROTEIN | 1.3G SALT

CHICKEN SATAY WITH SWEET POTATO AND SPINACH STIR-FRY

This seriously flavorful dish is packed with Asian punch, and the satay sauce has a mildly sweet and satisfying flavor.

SERVES: 4

PREP: 20 MINS PLUS MARINATING COOK: 20 MINS

8 small skinless and boneless chicken thighs (about 1¼ pounds), cut into ½-inch chunks

MARINADE

1 small lemon grass stalk, finely chopped
1 small shallot, finely chopped
1 large garlic clove, finely chopped
1 red chili, seeded and finely chopped
1-inch piece fresh ginger, peeled and finely chopped
2 tablespoons finely chopped fresh cilantro
2 tablespoons soy sauce
1 tablespoon peanut oil

PEANUT SATAY SAUCE

2 tablespoons unsweetened peanut butter
½ cup coconut milk

STIR-FRY

1 tablespoon peanut oil
½ red chili, seeded and thinly sliced
¾-inch piece fresh ginger, peeled and thinly sliced
1 large sweet potato, cut into strips using a vegetable peeler
7 cups baby spinach
dash of soy sauce

1. Soak eight bamboo skewers in water for at least 10 minutes.

2. Put all the marinade ingredients in a blender and process to a fine paste.

3. Put the chicken in a deep bowl. Scrape the marinade into the bowl and stir well so that all the chicken is thoroughly coated. Cover the bowl with plastic wrap and chill in the refrigerator for 2–4 hours.

4. To make the satay sauce, put the peanut butter and coconut milk in a bowl and stir well. Transfer to a dipping bowl.

5. Thread the marinated chicken evenly onto the skewers. Heat a ridged broiler pan over high heat until smoking hot. Cook the skewers for 2 minutes on each side, or until the chicken is cooked through and a little charred at the edges and the juices run clear with no sign of pink when a piece is cut in half.

6. Meanwhile, to make the stir-fry, heat the oil in a large wok over high heat. Add the chili and ginger and stir-fry for 30 seconds. Add the sweet potato and stir-fry for 1 minute, then add the spinach and soy sauce and stir-fry for 30 seconds.

7. Serve the skewers on a plate with the dipping sauce and individual servings of the stir-fry in bowls.

PER SERVING: 451 CALS | 26.6G FAT | 8.3G SAT FAT | 16.7G CARBS | 4.1G SUGARS | 4.2G FIBER | 35.7G PROTEIN | 2.2G SALT

MONKFISH IN PESTO AND PROSCIUTTO WITH RICOTTA SPINACH

Monkfish can dry out during cooking, but by wrapping it in prosciutto, you can keep it moist and add plenty of extra flavor and texture.

SERVES: 4

PREP: 25 MINS COOK: 25 MINS

8 prosciutto slices
3 tablespoons fresh green pesto
8 large fresh basil leaves
1¼ pounds monkfish tail, separated into 2 fillets
1 tablespoon olive oil

RICOTTA SPINACH

2 tablespoons olive oil
1 garlic clove, thinly sliced
5½ cups baby spinach
2 tablespoons ricotta cheese
sea salt and pepper, to taste

1. Preheat the oven to 350°F. Lay two large sheets of plastic wrap side-by-side on a work surface. Arrange the prosciutto slices on the plastic wrap so the long sides overlap by ½ inch. Spread the pesto all over the ham, leaving a ¾-inch border around the edge. Sprinkle the basil over the top.

2. Put one monkfish fillet on top of the pesto and basil, then lay the other fillet next to it the other way around, so its thick end is against its neighbor's thin end.

3. Fold the ham over the ends of the fish and then, using the plastic wrap, roll and encase the whole fillet tightly in the ham. Remove the plastic wrap. Transfer the parcel to a roasting pan so the seam in the ham is on the bottom, and lightly drizzle with the oil. Roast for 20–25 minutes, or until cooked through but still moist. Cover the pan with aluminum foil to keep the fish warm.

4. To make the ricotta spinach, heat the oil in a large skillet over medium-high heat. Add the garlic and cook for 30 seconds, or until it is soft but not burned. Stir in the spinach and cook, stirring all the time so the oil coats the leaves, for 1 minute, or until it is wilted but not completely collapsed. Transfer to a serving bowl, dot with blobs of the ricotta, and season well with salt and pepper.

5. Place the fish on a serving plate, carve into slices, and pour over any cooking juices from the roasting pan. Serve with the spinach.

MMM, MONKFISH

Monkfish is loaded with protein and includes vitamins B_6 and B_{12}, which are essential for brain function. It also includes the minerals phosphorus and selenium.

PER SERVING: 341 CALS | 22G FAT | 5G SAT FAT | 2.5G CARBS | 0.6G SUGARS | 0.8G FIBER | 35.2G PROTEIN | 2.3G SALT

CRISPY PARMESAN-COATED SEA BASS

Parmesan cheese, parsley, and lemon make a top-notch trio to spoon over sea bass, adding a delicious flavor without overpowering the delicate fish.

SERVES: 4
PREP: 15 MINS COOK: 4 MINS

3 tablespoons olive oil
4 sea bass fillets (about 4½ oz each), skin on and pin-boned
finely grated zest and juice of 1 unwaxed lemon, plus 1 lemon, cut into wedges to serve
1 cup finely grated Parmesan cheese
¼ cup finely chopped fresh flat-leaf parsley
sea salt and pepper, to taste
2½ cups watercress, arugula, or mixed leaves, to serve

1. Preheat the broiler to its highest setting. Brush the broiler rack with a little of the oil and lay the sea bass fillets on top, skin side down. Drizzle with a little of the remaining oil, give each fillet a good squeeze of lemon juice, and season with salt and pepper.

2. Put the lemon zest, cheese, and parsley in a bowl and mix well, then sprinkle the mixture evenly over the fish. Drizzle with the remaining oil.

3. Broil for 4 minutes, or until the fish is just cooked and golden—the exact cooking time will depend on the thickness of the fillets. Serve immediately with the salad and lemon wedges for squeezing over the fish.

PARMESAN PLEASE

Parmesan cheese is an excellent source of bone-building calcium and phosphorus. It also includes good levels of protein, vitamin B_{12}, zinc, selenium, and riboflavin.

PER SERVING: 339 CALS | 19.6G FAT | 6.3G SAT FAT | 2G CARBS | 0.5G SUGARS | 0.2G FIBER | 37G PROTEIN | 2G SALT

SQUID WITH SAFFRON MAYONNAISE

In this take on a classic squid dish, the celebrated crispy coating of the squid is made from cornstarch, which has a low sugar content.

SERVES: 2

PREP: 30 MINS COOK: 9 MINS

1 pound whole small squid, skinned, cleaned, and gutted
3 level tablespoons cornstarch
vegetable oil, for deep-frying
sea salt and pepper, to taste
2 lemon wedges, to serve (optional)

SAFFRON MAYONNAISE

small pinch of saffron strands
1 teaspoon lukewarm water
3 tablespoons mayonnaise
1/2 small garlic clove, finely chopped

SALAD

head of red endive, leaves separated
1 cup watercress or arugula
1/4 ounce Parmesan cheese, shaved
juice of 1/4 lemon
1 tablespoon extra-virgin olive oil

1. To make the saffron mayonnaise, put the saffron and water in a small bowl and let steep for 5 minutes. Stir during the soaking to release the flavor. Meanwhile, put the mayonnaise and garlic in a bowl and mix well. When the saffron has turned the water vibrant yellow, discard the saffron strands and stir the liquid into the mayonnaise. Transfer to two dipping bowls, cover with plastic wrap, and chill in the refrigerator.

COOKING SQUID

Smaller squid are often less tough than their large counterparts and require less cooking.

2. Preheat the oven to its lowest temperature. To make the salad, put the endive and watercress in a large bowl, then sprinkle with the cheese. Put the lemon juice and oil in a small bowl and mix well with a fork.

3. Slice the squid body into 1/4-inch circles and cut the tentacles in half. Wash under cold running water, then dry on paper towels. Put the cornstarch on a plate and season with salt and pepper, then toss the squid lightly in it to coat.

4. Heat the oil in a deep, heavy saucepan. To test whether it is hot enough, drop in a small cube of bread. If it takes about 30 seconds to turn golden, the oil is ready.

5. Cook the squid in two batches because too much squid in the pan will make the oil temperature drop. Sprinkle half the squid into the oil and cook for 2–3 minutes, until the coating is just tinged a golden color.

6. Using a slotted spoon, transfer the cooked squid to paper towels to drain, then keep warm in the oven while you cook the second batch.

7. Season the squid with salt and pepper. Pour the dressing over the salad. Serve the squid immediately with the salad and saffron mayonnaise, and lemon wedges for squeezing over the squid, if using.

PER SERVING: 783 CALS | 51.8G FAT | 8.4G SAT FAT | 35G CARBS | 2G SUGARS | 1.3G FIBER | 43.1G PROTEIN | 2.6G SALT

BAKED PUMPKIN AND CHEESE

This creamy, wholesome dip served in a pumpkin shell is loads of fun and will be loved by the whole family.

SERVES: 4
PREP: 15 MINS COOK: 1 HOUR 10 MINS

- 1 small pumpkin
- $1^1/_4$ cups heavy cream
- 3 garlic cloves, thinly sliced
- 1 tablespoon fresh thyme leaves, plus sprigs to garnish
- $4^1/_2$ ounces gruyère, swiss, or Muenster cheese
- sea salt and pepper, to taste
- 4 slices of whole-grain crusty bread, to serve
- $2^1/_2$ cups pepper salad greens, such as watercress or mâche, to serve (optional)

1. Preheat the oven to 350°F. Cut horizontally straight through the top quarter of the pumpkin to form a lid. Scoop out the seeds. Put the pumpkin in a large, deep ovenproof dish.

2. Put the cream and garlic in a saucepan, then place it over medium heat and bring to just below boiling point. Remove from the heat, season with salt and pepper, and stir in the thyme. Pour the mixture into the pumpkin and replace the pumpkin lid.

3. Bake for 1 hour, or until the flesh is tender. Be careful not to overcook the pumpkin, or it may collapse. Remove from the oven, lift off the lid, and sprinkle in the cheese. Bake for an additional 10 minutes with the lid off.

4. Sprinkle with the thyme sprigs and some of the salad, if using. Serve the soft pumpkin flesh with a generous helping of the cheesy cream, a slice of the bread, and the remaining salad, if using.

PUMPKIN POWER

Pumpkin is rich in beta-carotene, which the body converts into vitamin A, a powerful antioxidant that helps us maintain good skin and sight. It is also a good source of the B vitamins, including B_6 and folates.

PER SERVING: 453 CALS | 38G FAT | 23.3G SAT FAT | 18.4G CARBS | 3.5G SUGARS | 1.2G FIBER | 13.3G PROTEIN | 1.8G SALT

BUTTERNUT SQUASH AND LENTIL STEW

Brown lentils have a powerful flavor and are a great choice for vegetarians and meat-eaters alike. They are also rich in iron and protein.

SERVES: 4
PREP: 10 MINS COOK: 30 MINS

1 tablespoon olive oil
1 onion, finely chopped
3 garlic cloves, finely chopped
2 tablespoons tomato paste
2 teaspoons ground cumin
1 teaspoon ground cinnamon
1/4 teaspoon cayenne pepper
1 butternut squash, peeled, seeded, and cut into cubes
1/2 cup brown lentils
2 cups vegetable stock
juice of 1/4 lemon
sea salt and pepper, to taste

TO SERVE
2 tablespoons finely chopped fresh cilantro
2 tablespoons slivered almonds
1/4 cup plain yogurt

1. Heat the oil in a large saucepan over medium–high heat. Add the onion and garlic and cook, stirring occasionally, for 5 minutes, or until soft.

2. Add the tomato paste, cumin, cinnamon, and cayenne and season well with salt and pepper, then stir. Add the squash, lentils, and stock and bring to a boil. Reduce the heat to low and simmer uncovered, stirring occasionally, for 25 minutes, or until the squash and lentils are tender.

3. Just before serving, stir in the lemon juice. Serve hot, sprinkled with the cilantro and almonds, with a dollop of the yogurt on top.

LOVELY LENTILS

Lentils contain high levels of soluble fiber, which studies show can help to reduce the risk of heart disease. They are also rich in protein, folate, and magnesium.

PER SERVING: 234 CALS | 7G FAT | 1.1G SAT FAT | 35G CARBS | 6G SUGARS | 11G FIBER | 9.7G PROTEIN | 2.6G SALT

NEW POTATO, FETA, AND HERB FRITTATA

This easy-to-make treat is perfect for a main dish, or let it stand until cold, then wrap it in aluminum foil and enjoy for lunch or take on a picnic.

SERVES: 4

PREP: 20 MINS COOK: 35 MINS

- 9 ounces new potatoes, scrubbed
- 3 cups baby spinach
- 5 eggs
- 1 tablespoon finely chopped fresh dill, plus extra to garnish
- 1 tablespoon snipped fresh chives, plus extra to garnish
- 4 ounces feta cheese, crumbled
- 1/2 tablespoon butter
- 1 tablespoon olive oil
- sea salt and pepper, to taste

1. Cook the potatoes in a large saucepan of lightly salted boiling water for 25 minutes, or until tender.

2. Put the spinach in a colander and drain the potatoes over the top to wilt it. Set aside until cool enough to handle.

3. Cut the potatoes lengthwise into slices 1/4 inch thick. Squeeze the excess water from the spinach.

4. Crack the eggs into a bowl and lightly beat with a fork. Add the dill and chives and beat again. Season with pepper and add three-quarters of the feta. Preheat the broiler to high.

5. Heat the butter and oil together in an ovenproof 8-inch skillet over medium heat until melted and foaming. Add the potatoes and spinach and cook, stirring, for 1 minute. Pour in the egg mixture. Cook, stirring, for 2 minutes, or until half set, then cook for an additional 3–4 minutes without stirring, until set and golden brown underneath.

6. Sprinkle with the remaining feta, then broil for 2 minutes, until golden brown on top. Serve hot or cold, sprinkled with the remaining dill and chives.

EXCELLENT EGGS

Eggs are a wonderful source of protein, vitamins A and D, and the B vitamins.

PER SERVING: 272 CALS | 18.3G FAT | 8.2G SAT FAT | 12.3G CARBS | 2.2G SUGARS | 2G FIBER | 14.5G PROTEIN | 1.9G SALT

DESSERTS AND BAKING

LEMON CHEESECAKE WITH ALMOND CRUST

A zesty and creamy cheesecake with a crunchy crust that's perfect for when friends come over for dinner.

SERVES: 8

PREP: 20 MINS COOK: 1 HOUR

1½ tablespoons butter, plus extra for greasing
1 cup ground almonds (almond meal)
½ cup finely chopped almonds
2 tablespoons smooth sugar-free almond butter
2 tablespoons quinoa flour
2 tablespoons stevia

TOPPING

1 cup mascarpone cheese
1¼ cups cream cheese
2 extra-large eggs
finely grated zest and juice of 1 large unwaxed lemon
1 tablespoon quinoa flour
¼ cup stevia

1. Preheat the oven to 350°F. Lightly butter an 8-inch round nonstick springform cake pan and line the bottom with parchment paper.
2. To make the crust, melt the butter in a small saucepan over medium-low heat. Pour it into a large bowl and add the ground almonds, chopped almonds, almond butter, quinoa flour, and stevia, then mix well. Spoon the mixture into the prepared pan and, using the back of a fork, press down into an even layer. Bake for 25 minutes, then remove from the oven and reduce the temperature to 250°F.
3. To make the topping, put the mascarpone cheese and cream cheese in a large bowl and whisk until loose. Beat for an additional 30 seconds, then add the eggs, one at a time, beating between each addition. Add the lemon zest and juice, quinoa flour, and stevia, then whisk again until well mixed.
4. Pour the topping over the crust. Bake for 50 minutes, or until the sides are set and the middle still has a slight wobble. Leave to cool, then cover and chill in the refrigerator for 1–2 hours.

LOVE YOUR LEMONS

If your lemons are old and hard, put them in the microwave on high for 30 seconds—this makes them easier to zest and juice.

PER SERVING: 402 CALS | 35.6G FAT | 16.2G SAT FAT | 11G CARBS | 3.7G SUGARS | 2.4G FIBER | 10.6G PROTEIN | 0.5G SALT

PUMPKIN PIE WITH PECANS

Pumpkin pie is ideal for a dinner party or cozy family lunch. The almond pastry adds a sweet nuttiness.

SERVES: 8

PREP: 35 MINS COOK: 1 HOUR

PASTRY DOUGH

3/4 cup ground almonds (almond meal)
1 1/2 tablespoons butter, diced
1 tablespoon coconut flour
1 tablespoon stevia
1 egg
pinch of sea salt

FILLING

6 cups peeled, seeded, and diced pumpkin or butternut squash
2 tablespoons coconut flour
2 tablespoons stevia
1 1/2 teaspoons ground cinnamon
1 teaspoon freshly grated nutmeg
1 1/2 tablespoons butter, diced
2 eggs
3 tablespoons heavy cream
2 tablespoons coarsely chopped pecans

1. Preheat the oven to 325°F. Line a 9-inch fluted, nonstick tart pan with parchment paper.

2. To make the pastry dough, put all the ingredients in a food processor and process until it forms a soft dough. Press the dough into the prepared pan, pushing it up the sides so it evenly covers the bottom. Prick all over with a fork. Bake for 15 minutes, or until the sides are golden. Set aside to cool.

3. Meanwhile, to make the filling, cook the pumpkin in a large saucepan of lightly salted boiling water for 10 minutes, or until soft. Drain, then let cool. Put the coconut flour, stevia, cinnamon, nutmeg, and pumpkin in a food processor and process until smooth. Add the butter, eggs, and cream and process again. Transfer the filling to the tart shell.

4. Sprinkle with the pecans. Bake for 55–60 minutes, or until the sides are set and the center still has a slight wobble. Serve warm or cold.

LINING A TIN MADE EASY

To make parchment paper really pliable, crumple it up before you use it; all the creases will then fit easily into the fluted edge of the pan.

PER SERVING: 224 CALS | 19.1G FAT | 8.4G SAT FAT | 9.5G CARBS | 2.2G SUGARS | 2.6G FIBER | 6.4G PROTEIN | 0.3G SALT

MOCHA SOUFFLÉS WITH MASCARPONE

A soufflé is the most glamorous of desserts, puffing up when it comes out of the oven and collapsing before the eyes of the diner.

SERVES: 4
PREP: 15 MINS COOK: 15 MINS

2 teaspoons butter, to grease
2 tablespoons ground almonds (almond meal)
1 tablespoon unsweetened cocoa powder, plus a little extra to dust
1 tablespoon prepared strong espresso
small pinch of sea salt
1/3 cup cold water
3 egg whites
1 tablespoon rice malt syrup
1/4 cup mascarpone cheese, to serve

1. Preheat the oven to 375°F. Lightly butter four ramekins, then sprinkle with the ground almonds. Roll and rotate the ramekins so the almonds stick to the butter, coating all sides.

2. Put the cocoa powder, espresso, salt, and water into a small saucepan and cook, stirring over low heat, until smooth. Increase the heat to medium-high and bring to a boil, then cook for an additional 1 minute. Pour the mixture into a large bowl and let cool.

3. Put the egg whites in a separate large, clean glass bowl and whisk until they form soft peaks. Add the rice malt syrup and whisk again until you have stiff peaks. Using a metal spoon, gently fold a spoonful of the egg white into the cocoa mixture, preserving as much air as possible, then fold in the rest.

4. Spoon the mixture into the prepared ramekins. Bake for 10–12 minutes, or until the soufflés are towering out of the ramekins.

5. Add a tablespoon of mascarpone to each ramekin and sprinkle with cocoa powder. Serve immediately, before the soufflés start to collapse.

SOUFFLÉ TIPS

For successful soufflés, it's a good idea to have everything measured out before you start. Make sure all equipment is clean and grease-free and all ingredients are at room temperature. Don't open the oven door while the soufflés cook.

PER SERVING: 172 CALS | 15.1G FAT | 9.1G SAT FAT | 5G CARBS | 2.7G SUGARS | 0.9G FIBER | 4.9G PROTEIN | 0.5G SALT

CHOCOLATE-LIME DESSERTS

Small and rich, these decadent chocolate and zesty lime desserts make a rich yet surprisingly refreshing end to a meal.

SERVES: 4

PREP: 10 MINS COOK: 8 MINUTES CHILL: 4 HOURS

1 cup heavy cream
1½ tablespoons rice malt syrup
1 ounce bittersweet chocolate, broken into pieces
finely grated zest of 1 lime, plus 1½ tablespoons juice
1 teaspoon unsweetened cocoa powder

1. Put the cream in a saucepan and slowly bring to a boil over medium heat. Add the rice malt syrup and stir well, then boil for 3 minutes. Stir in the chocolate, most of the lime zest, and all the lime juice until the chocolate has melted.

2. Pour the mixture into four espresso cups. Cover with plastic wrap and chill in the refrigerator for at least 4 hours.

3. Decorate the desserts with the cocoa powder and remaining lime zest and serve.

ALSO TRY THIS

If you would prefer these desserts a little less rich, then leave out the chocolate.

PER SERVING: 276 CALS | 26G FAT | 16.3G SAT FAT | 9.4G CARBS | 3.8G SUGARS | 1G FIBER | 2G PROTEIN | TRACE SALT

ZUCCHINI LOAF CAKE WITH CREAM CHEESE FROSTING

Zucchini cake is just as delicious as carrot cake. It's super moist, with a creamy and fresh flavor.

SERVES: 10

PREP: 25 MINS COOK: 1 HOUR

1 3/4 cups ground almonds (almond meal)
1/2 teaspoon baking powder
1/2 teaspoon baking soda
3 tablespoons stevia
1/3 cup chopped mixed nuts
4 tablespoons butter
2 extra-large eggs, beaten
1 teaspoon vanilla extract
2 cups shredded zucchini

FROSTING

1 cup cream cheese
1 tablespoon stevia
finely grated zest and juice of 1/4 unwaxed lemon

1. Preheat the oven to 325°F. Line a nonstick loaf pan with parchment paper.

2. Put the ground almonds, baking powder, baking soda, stevia, and half the nuts in a large bowl and stir well.

3. Melt the butter in a small saucepan over medium-low heat. Pour it onto the dry ingredients. Add the eggs, vanilla, and zucchini, and mix well.

4. Spoon the batter into the prepared pan and spread it into an even layer. Bake for 55–60 minutes, or until well risen and a toothpick comes out clean when inserted into the center of the cake. Let cool for 15 minutes, then remove from the pan, peel off the parchment paper, and transfer to a wire rack.

5. To make the frosting, put the cream cheese and stevia in a large bowl and whisk until light and airy. Add the lemon zest and juice, and whisk again briefly. Using a spatula, spread the frosting over the top of the cake. Decorate with the remaining nuts and serve.

UNWAXED LEMONS

If you are intending to use the zest, it is important to buy unwaxed lemons. If you can't find them, scrub the lemons well before use. Choose firm, heavy lemons with a thick, knobbly skin that has no tinges of green.

PER SERVING: 237 CALS | 21.9G FAT | 6.5G SAT FAT | 5.3G CARBS | 2.2G SUGARS | 2.4G FIBER | 7.2G PROTEIN | 0.6G SALT

SWEET POTATO BROWNIES

Sweet potatoes make gooey, sweet brownies. Once you have tried these, you are sure to bake them again and again!

MAKES: 12 BROWNIES

PREP: 30 MINS   COOK: 20 MINS

- 2/3 cup olive oil, plus extra to grease
- 1 sweet potato, coarsely grated
- 3/4 cup stevia
- 2/3 cup unsweetened cocoa powder
- 1/2 teaspoon baking powder
- 1/2 teaspoon baking soda
- 1/2 cup ground almonds (almond meal)
- 2 eggs, beaten
- 1/4 cup coarsely chopped walnuts

1. Preheat the oven to 350°F. Lightly oil a shallow 8-inch square cake pan, then line it with a large square of parchment paper, snipping into the corners diagonally, then pressing the paper into the pan so that the bottom and sides are lined.

2. Put all the ingredients in a large bowl and stir well. Pour the batter into the prepared pan. Bake for 20 minutes, or until well risen and the center is only just set.

3. Let cool in the pan for 15 minutes. Lift out of the pan using the parchment paper, then carefully remove the paper. Cut into 12 brownies to serve.

ALSO TRY THIS

If this recipe is too chocolaty for your taste, reduce the amount of cocoa to 1/3 cup.

PER BROWNIE: 182 CALS | 17.2G FAT | 2.6G SAT FAT | 6.6G CARBS | 1G SUGARS | 2.4G FIBER | 3.4G PROTEIN | 0.2G SALT

REALLY RICH AVOCADO CHOCOLATE MOUSSE

Avocados add creaminess and richness to this delicious mousse, while chocolate is decadent and flavorful—wonderful!

SERVES: 4

PREP: 10 MINS

2 ripe avocados, peeled, pitted, and coarsely chopped
1/3 cup unsweetened cocoa powder
2 tablespoons rice malt syrup
1 teaspoon vanilla extract
small pinch of sea salt
2 tablespoons unsweetened almond milk

1. Put all the ingredients in a blender or food processor and process until combined. Scrape down the sides and process for an additional minute, or until the mousse is airy. If it is still too thick, add a splash more almond milk and process again briefly.

2. Spoon the mousse into small teacups or serving bowls and serve immediately, or cover and chill in the refrigerator for up to 4 hours.

RIPENING AVOCADOS

If your avocados are too hard, put them in a sealed paper bag with a ripe tomato for 24 hours and they should ripen to perfection.

PER SERVING: 151 CALS | 11.8G FAT | 2.1G SAT FAT | 15G CARBS | 2.7G SUGARS | 7.5G FIBER | 3G PROTEIN | 0.4G SALT

VANILLA PANNA COTTA WITH PISTACHIOS AND ROSE WATER

Panna cotta is an elegant dessert. Here, the dairy milk is replaced by unsweetened almond milk, which complements the fragrant rose water and emerald pistachios.

SERVES: 4

PREP: 15 MINS COOK: 4 MINS CHILL: 2 HOURS

3 sheets / 1 (1/4 oz) package powdered gelatin
1 1/4 cups heavy cream
1 cup unsweetened almond milk
1 vanilla bean, split lengthwise
2 tablespoons stevia
2 tablespoons rose water
2 tablespoons unsalted pistachios, coarsely chopped

1. Soak the gelatin in a shallow bowl of cold water for 5–10 minutes, or until floppy.

2. Meanwhile, pour the cream and almond milk into a large, heavy saucepan. Scrape in the vanilla seeds using a sharp knife, then drop in the pod. Bring to a boil over medium-high heat, stirring from time to time. Let cool for 5 minutes, then stir in the stevia and, using a fork, remove the vanilla bean.

3. Squeeze the water out of the gelatin and stir the gelatin into the custard until dissolved. Pour the custard into four ramekins, then let cool for 15 minutes. Cover with plastic wrap and chill in the refrigerator for at least 2 hours, or overnight if you have the time.

4. Fill a bowl halfway with boiling water. Dip each ramekin into the water briefly, making sure it doesn't splash over the top, then turn out onto serving plates. Drizzle the panna cottas with the rose water and sprinkle with the pistachios.

USING GELATIN

It is important the mixture cools to lukewarm before you add the gelatin; if the heat is too high, the gelatin won't set the dessert. Test it with your finger.

PER SERVING: 313 CALS | 31.1G FAT | 17.6G SAT FAT | 4.2G CARBS | 0.5G SUGARS | 0.8G FIBER | 6.2G PROTEIN | 0.1G SALT

BAKED PASSION FRUIT CUSTARDS

Light and fluffy with a refreshing tropical flavor, this simple dessert tastes every bit as good as it looks.

SERVES: 4
PREP: 15 MINS COOK: 45 MINS

2 passion fruit
4 extra-large eggs
3/4 cup coconut milk
3 tablespoons stevia
1 teaspoon orange flower water

1. Preheat the oven to 350°F. Halve the passion fruit, scoop out the flesh from three of the halves, and push it through a strainer using the back of a spoon to remove the seeds.

2. Crack the eggs into a large bowl. Add the passion fruit juice, coconut milk, stevia, and orange flower water, and whisk until smooth and airy.

3. Pour the passion fruit custard into four ramekins, place them in a roasting pan, and pour in hot water to reach halfway up the dishes. Bake for 40–45 minutes, or until just set.

4. Scoop the pulp from the remaining passion fruit half and spoon a little onto each dish. Serve immediately, or cover with plastic wrap and chill in the refrigerator for up to 8 hours.

PASSION FRUIT

Passion fruit is an excellent source of fiber and vitamins A and C, which help boost the immune system.

PER SERVING: 185 CALS | 15.4G FAT | 10.2G SAT FAT | 3.8G CARBS | 2.5G SUGARS | 0.9G FIBER | 9G PROTEIN | 0.2G SALT

RASPBERRY AND MASCARPONE ICE CREAM

Fresh raspberries and extra creaminess from the mascarpone mean you will be fighting people off the last scoops of this classic ice cream.

SERVES: 8

PREP: 20 MINS COOK: 10 MINS FREEZE: 4 HOURS

- 1 extra-large egg, plus 4 extra-large egg yolks
- $2\frac{1}{2}$ tablespoons stevia
- $\frac{1}{2}$ cup mascarpone cheese
- 1 teaspoon vanilla extract
- $1\frac{2}{3}$ cups heavy cream
- $\frac{3}{4}$ cup raspberries, halved

1. Crack the egg into a large heatproof bowl, add the yolks and stevia, and whisk with an electric handheld mixer for 30 seconds. Place over a saucepan of gently simmering water, making sure the bowl doesn't touch the water, and whisk until the mixture is pale and airy. This cooks the eggs and makes a sweet custard, but be careful not to overcook them.

2. Pour cold water into a bowl and put the custard bowl into it, so the bottom of the custard bowl is cooling in the water. Continue to whisk for 2 minutes, then lift the bowl out of the water and set aside.

3. Put the mascarpone and vanilla in another large bowl and whisk briefly until loose. Pour in the cream and whisk again until it forms soft peaks.

4. Using a metal spoon, gently fold the custard into the cream mixture, preserving as much air as possible. Stir in the raspberries.

5. Pour the mixture into a freezeproof container, cover with a lid, and freeze for 4 hours, or until set. Take the ice cream out of the freezer 10 minutes before you serve it to let it soften. Scoop it into glasses or small bowls and serve.

ALSO TRY THIS

If you prefer vanilla ice cream, simply leave out the raspberries.

PER SERVING: 285 CALS | 28.6G FAT | 16.5G SAT FAT | 3.9G CARBS | 1.2G SUGARS | 0.8G FIBER | 4.2G PROTEIN | 0.1G SALT

CHOCOLATE AND CHERRY SORBET

The chocolate makes this sorbet rich and thick, while the frozen cherries add instant glamor.

SERVES: 4

PREP: 10 MINS COOK: 10 MINS FREEZE: 4 HOURS

1¼ cups cold water
3 tablespoons stevia
¼ cup cocoa powder
¼ teaspoon ground allspice
4 cherries, pitted and chopped, plus 4 whole cherries to decorate
2½ ounces bittersweet chocolate, broken into small pieces

1. Pour the water into a saucepan, then add the stevia, cocoa powder, allspice, and chopped cherries. Whisk lightly, then slowly bring to a boil over medium-high heat.

2. Remove the pan from the heat and let cool for 2–3 minutes. Stir in the chocolate, then pour the mixture into a freezeproof container, cover with a lid, and freeze for 4 hours, or until set. Stir with a fork every 30 minutes to break up the ice crystals. Put the four whole cherries in the freezer too.

3. Take the sorbet out of the freezer 10 minutes before you serve to let it soften. Scoop it into glasses or small bowls, decorate with a frozen cherry, and serve.

DARK CHOCOLATE

Tests have found that dark chocolate is packed with antioxidants and polyphenols, which are thought to protect the body from some cancers and heart conditions.

PER SERVING: 129 CALS | 8.3G FAT | 4.7G SAT FAT | 14.3G CARBS | 6.3G SUGARS | 4.4G FIBER | 2.6G PROTEIN | TRACE SALT

FROZEN YOGURT CUPS

Containing calcium-rich yogurt and heart-protecting berries, these little confections are good for you and a really tasty summer treat.

MAKES: 12

PREP: 10 MINS FREEZE: 2 HOURS

2 cups plain yogurt
finely grated zest of 1/2 orange
2 cups mixed raspberries, blueberries, and hulled and halved or quartered strawberries
12 fresh mint sprigs, to decorate

1. Line a 12-section muffin pan with paper liners.
2. Put the yogurt and orange zest in a large bowl and mix well. Add two-thirds of the strawberries, blueberries, and raspberries, and mix well.
3. Spoon the mixture into the paper cases. Freeze for 2 hours, or until just frozen. Decorate with the remaining berries and the mint sprigs, and serve.

SAY YES TO YOGURT

Flavored yogurts tend to be full of sugar, so mixing fruit into plain yogurt is a great solution.

PER SERVING: 33.7 CALS | 1.2G FAT | 0.8G SAT FAT | 4G CARBS | 2.7G SUGARS | 0.7G FIBER | 1.4G PROTEIN | TRACE SALT

INDEX